# Handbook for Teaching Physical Sciences

# Handbook for Teaching Physical Sciences
## Methods and Techniques

Dr. M.T.V. NAGARAJU
*Assistant Professor*
Department of Education
Sri Krishnadevaraya University
ANANTAPUR (A.P.)

KANISHKA PUBLISHERS, DISTRIBUTORS
NEW DELHI-110 002

**KANISHKA PUBLISHERS, DISTRIBUTORS**
4697/5-21 A, Ansari Road, Daryaganj
New Delhi-110 002
Phones : 2327 0497, 2328 8285
Fax : 011-2328 8285
E-mail: kanishka_publishing@yahoo.co.in

*Handbook for Teaching Physical Sciences*
First Published 2008

ISBN 978-81-8457-062-5

PRINTED IN INDIA

Published by Madan Sachdeva for Kanishka Publishers, Distributors, 4697/5-21A, Ansari Road, Daryaganj, New Delhi-110 002, Typeset by Sunshine Graphics, Delhi, and Printed at Nice Printing Press, Delhi.

# Preface

Science has helped us to understand the operation and behaviour of the atmosphere which surrounds the earth. It has been found that the earth is neither a significant part of the universe nor the centre of it. Today the Science makes the drastic changes in the society.

As a part of learning, Science is a compulsory subject at secondary level apart with the Mathematics and Social Studies. Never day students felt that science is a subject systematically learn and understand with the surrounding environment.

The change has been takes place in the schools with the class teachers. Teaching science requires a shift in emphasis. The science lessons must be inserted in the standard curriculum and regularly reinforced to encourage habits of mind. Basis on the above requirements the author thought that it is very important to know the teacher how to transact the science subject in the classroom. For that a teacher trainee requires some amount of potential in transacting the subject in the classroom.

The present volume of handbook provides the trainee a comprehensive overview of the modern approaches and strategies in science teaching and raises the questions namely:

- What is science?
- How far is it relevant to the individual and society?
- What types of methods and techniques those are required to deal the classroom effectively?
- How should we inculcate the scientific skills and teaching skills among the trainees?
- When we evaluate the students and how?

For answering the entire questions, the author made an attempt and clearly given a picture of knowledge in the *Handbook for Teaching Physical Sciences*.

# Contents

# Contents

# 1
# Nature of Science

## Introduction

The present day world is considered as a scientific world, as we are all living in an environment that is completely surrounded by scientific advances and their application. We cannot imagine the present day world without science. Life becomes miserable without science and it horrifies even to think in that direction. We are very much dependent on the present day utensils and gadgets based on the application of science.

Scientific knowledge, concepts and our understanding of the methods and implications of science have been growing over the past few thousand years; the developments have been most rapid and spectacular over the past few hundred years. In the earlier phases of development many phenomena and areas of observation were treated as being distinct and separate. As knowledge and understanding improved, one began to see unifying elements, which brought together what might otherwise have been, regarded as disparate fields.

You must be studying, learning, using and applying science from the beginning of your formal education until now. You may be a Bachelor of Science or Master of Science. During your more than one and half decades of formal education and your day-to-day life you must have learnt so many things about science and their application in day-to-day life. But did you ever ask yourself about "what exactly do I mean by science?" I feel that you have not done this exercise before. As you are going to be a teacher of Physical

Sciences, a thorough understanding about the term "Science" is a must as it is going to influence your way of teaching.

A teacher of physical science should learn the vast mass of scientific knowledge in different fields in terms of basic concepts, such as space, time, energy, change, information and so on. It is surprising to see broadly logical similarities in areas of physical, chemical and biological sciences and the concepts are inter-related in an overall manner. We should learn the conceptual framework science, which is usually the weakest element in our current teaching related to science.

In this chapter you are going to learn about various definitions and meaning of science. You are also going to study its structure, which is very crucial in differentiating it from other subjects. Finally, you are also going to study about the scope and importance of science.

**Definitions and Meaning of Science**

***Definition of Science***

Human beings have been trying to understand the nature around them by making an effective use of their senses and their ability to communicate to accumulate and organise the information.

This systematised store of human knowledge gained after generalising and inter-relating the isolated facts is known as science.

The word 'science' has been originated from a Latin word "scientia", which means 'knowledge'. Science in general has been defined in so many different ways. Some definitions are given below:

"Science is a systematised body of knowledge."
"Science is nothing but organised common sense."
"Science is an interpretation of natural phenomena."

Oxford Advanced Learners Dictionary defines science as "An organised knowledge, especially when obtained by observation and testing of facts, about the physical world, natural laws and society."

The Columbia Encyclopaedia defines science as "An accumulated and systematised learning in general us age restricted to natural phenomena."

John Woodburn and E. O. Obourn consider science as "That human endeavour that seeks to describe with even increasing accuracy, the events and circumstances, which occur or exist within our natural environment."

Fitzpatrick – Policies for Science Education defines science, as "Science is a cumulative and endless series of empirical observations, which result in the formation of concepts and theories, with both concepts and theories being subject to modification in the light of further empirical observations. Science is both a body of knowledge and the process of acquiring and refining knowledge."

## Meaning of Science

From the above definitions we can understand that science is simultaneously a body of knowledge and the continuous, self-evaluative process of enquiry. Some scientists have thought of as being an addition to knowledge, the process by which information is obtained and verified.

### *Static View*

The static view places science in the centre of the stage the present inter-connected set of principles, laws and theories together with the vast array of systematised information.

### *Dynamic View*

In contrast to the static view, this regards science as an activity thus; the present state of knowledge is of importance chiefly as a basis for further operations. Science is a large and ever-increasing *body of scientific knowledge* and also a package of *processes* by which we can increase our knowledge of external world. There are – facts, theories, concepts and also a way of working, which together constitute 'the subject science'. Thus, science is not just content. Science is content plus processes. This is dual nature of science.

## Structure of Science

It has been observed that many of the school-going children have not been experiencing science in its real sense. Science comprises of its substantive (content) and syntactical (process) structures. The former belongs to its terms, concepts, conceptual schemes, theories, generalisations, laws and principles, while the latter belong to its processes, i.e., observation, measurement, inference and interpretation. Cognitive constructivists emphasise that children construct their own meanings by interacting with the objects, etc. In order to nurture science talent of the children, it is therefore, suggested that they be tunnelled through inquiry activities. Hence, science education of the school-going children had to reflect its substantive as well as its syntactical structures.

### 1. *Substantive Stucture of Science*

The substantive structure of science engages students in the process of enquiring scientific realities or actual, permanent or genuine knowledge of science. The substantive structure of science embraces its terms like facts, concepts, conceptual schemes, hypotheses, theories, generalisations, principles and laws that govern understanding of its realities.

Hence, science can be expressed as a body of knowledge.

(i) *Science as a Body of Knowledge:* Scientific information is often factually presented. If we consider facts as truths therefore indisputable but relatively few facts are presented. Most scientific information is presented in the form of generalisations, which sum up facts. In addition much is presented in the form of hypotheses, theories and laws.

- *Facts:* A fact is a truth. So far science is concerned, this would have to be a demonstrable truth or this is a happening in time or space. Scientific facts can be recognised when they are obviously the products of direct observation. It is a statement of an actual event or a physical object. It is mostly empirical in nature.
  *Eg. Water changes to steam when boiled.*
  Iron expands on heating
- *Generalisations:* As facts accumulate they may begin to show certain relationships. Descriptions of these relationships are called generalisations. They are powerful tools for bringing raw data into a comprehensive whole.
  *Eg. Matter Occupies space.*
- *Concepts:* A concept is a generalised idea suggested to the individual by object, symbol or situation. Concepts vary from simple to complex, they have definitions. Concept learning involves processes of learning and is more than memorisation. Concepts are the basis of abstract thinking.

*Eg. Work, Temperature, Elasticity, Atoms combine to from molecules, etc.*

- *Hypotheses and theories:* Facts are always added but never discarded and generalisations, which are constantly being defined, the speculations of science are always in a state of flux being amended, discarded and replaced.
  Theories are rather conclusions based on the previous knowledge, hypotheses and some mathematical calculations.
  *Eg. Atomic theories*
- *Principles and Laws:* It is a generalised statement through which unrelated data is systematised. Generalisations that are passed upon a large number of observations, all consistent with in the limits of observational error and are often treated as certainties. We label them as principles or laws.
  *Eg. Newton's Laws, Archimedes Principle etc.*

**2. *Syntactic Structure of Science***

By syntactical constituent of science is meant the process of scientific inquiry. The process of science includes observation, measurement, drawing of an inference, generation of a hypothesis and/ or a prediction and their experimental testing, interpretation of empirical/ intuitive observation and making of a mental model of scientific reality.

Hence, science can be expressed as a process of investigation and a way of thinking.

(i) *Science as a Process of Investigation:* Science begins with gathering and cataloguing of facts. These are arranged and given meaning so that predictions can be made. The resulting speculations must be tested and new conclusions made.
The process of science is expressed in terms of "science is what scientists do." But in order to understand this statement we have to understand how scientists work. There are at least three basic things that the scientists do. They are:
- *Scientists Make Descriptions of Phenomena:* The scientists in different fields search for the answers to the

questions such as—What is? How many? How much? How long? When? Where? Under what circumstances? etc. The scientists try to describe phenomena in nature and establish relationships. In order to do that they use what we call the "scientific method."

- *Scientists Make Explanations:* The scientists after having described an event or phenomenon attempt to find out the 'reason' or why such event and phenomena occur the way they do. This usually involves careful observation of interactions and inter-relationships between different things and the conditions under which such phenomena occur.
- *Scientists Make Predictions:* Scientists use ideas of their own or of others as tools for testing and gaining knowledge. They use many resources to get valid answers to their questions and problems. They design their own experiments and invent new tools with which they observe and check different phenomena.

The current innovations in schools emphasise the processes of science, the ways in which scientists advance their knowledge and solve problems, if you as a science teacher, are to engage your pupils in the processes of science, it is important that you should have thought carefully about what these processes are. The sequence of development of these processes is as follows:

1. Observing
2. Classifying
3. Using numbers
4. Measuring
5. Using space-time relationships
6. Communicating
7. Predicting
8. Inferring
9. Defining operationally
10. Formulating Hypotheses
11. Interpreting Data
12. Controlling Variables and
13. Experimenting.

(ii) *Science as a Way of Thinking:* This involves the thinking process based on empirical basis, objectivity, assumptions, inductive—deductive reasoning, and analytical and synthetic approach, cause and effect relationships.

Hence from the above discussion science can be defined as "The process by which we increase and refine understanding of ourselves and of the universe through continuous observation, experimentation, application and verification." It can be concluded that:

*(i)* Science is a process as well as a product of the process. In process from it suggests the ways and means of exploring truth and in its product from it presents a systematic and organised body of useful knowledge.

*(ii)* The process form of knowledge (syntactical) is more important than its product from as the way of exploring truth and acquiring knowledge is always given more preference in science than were memorisation of the accumulated facts.

*(iii)* Science always remains in search of truth and the scientific truths can never be taken as absolutely and permanently true. Thus science by nature is dynamic but not static.

*(iv)* The method or procedure adopted by science in the explanation of truth is quite unique and distinct from the methods adopted in such a study by other subjects. This is known as the 'Scientific Method.'

*(v)* The study of science brings a typical change in the attitude of its readers and development of such attitude is known as 'Scientific Attitude.'

## Scope and Importance of Science

### *Scope of Science*

People tend to think of science as dealing with the natural world as distinct from the other worlds of music, art, literature, etc. Thus it includes physics, chemistry, botany, zoology, geology, astronomy, etc., which do not deal with man and his operations.

Some limit science to those subjects that are empirical in nature i.e., that deal with facts obtained by the direct observation of nature. This admits parts and not all of psychology, anthropology, sociology, economics and even history.

So a subject is a part of science if empirical data can be obtained, used as a basis for hypotheses and tested objectively.

***Importance of Science***

The importance of science has been thoroughly understood by the whole world and that's why we are all saying that we are in the scientific age. Its importance can be explained with an array of so many examples. In brief it can be explained in the following words:

Science and technology have become the backbone of today's development in all the fields. It helps us to understand the nature and life around us and lead a comfortable life and pleasant life.

A citizen of a modern world sees the countless manifestations of science all around him. There is no aspect of man's life today, which has not been influenced by science in one-way or other. This is because we are living in an age of scientific culture. Science has shrunk the world and totally changed the human outlook. In fact, science now has an all-pervading influence on every sphere of human activity. Further, modern science is no longer confined to the surface of this globe; its sphere of achievements has gone beyond the earth.

In recent times, there has been rapid addition of knowledge to the world of science. Great advancements of science, technology and use of these scientific achievements in promoting the well-being of mankind through their application in the fields of industry, communication, transport, engineering, agriculture, medicine, information technology, space, etc., has made science more important than ever before. In addition to the immense and far-reaching material benefits of science, as the Indian Education puts it "... but even more profound is its contribution to culture. Science is liberating and enriching the mind and enlarging the human spirit. Its fundamental characteristic has turned out to be the unlimited growth. Every advance in science deepens our understanding of nature but it also heightens the sense of ignorance. Nature is inexhaustibly knowable. Nothing comparable to the scientific revolution in its impact on man's development and outlook has happened since the Neolithic times."

A detailed study of the importance of science will be discussed in the next chapter under the headings Impact of Science and Technology on Society and the Values of Teaching Science, which will enlighten us to a greater extent.

**Science Process Skills**

Educative process acts as a means to bring about certain developments, among children in cognitive, affective and psychomotor domains. It is the process by which children would be able to increase their understanding about the universe through continuous observation, experimentation, application and verification. In these days of rapid expansion of scientific and technological knowledge, the role of science education is paramount in developing scientific insights among children. The teaching-learning programmes at school level should emphasise on the acquisition of science process skills through science teaching. The learner generates the learning outcomes through the use of science process skills. In order to initiate better learning outcomes, it is necessary to train a child in using science process skills.

The current innovations in schools emphasise the processes of science, the way in which scientists advance their knowledge and solve problems. Science should be presented to pupils as a way in which they can conduct an inquiry into the nature of things as well as a body of information built by the other people. In the past, the processes, have neglected, and school science has been concerned almost exclusively with the 'body of information', the concepts, principles and techniques developed by scientists. Very rarely pupils are encouraged to become personally involved in solving problems, in discovering some science for themselves.

The teachers' guides of most recently developed school science programmes in United States and United Kingdom suggest ways in which pupils can become involved in scientific inquiry. They are asked to follow the stages: Problem – Hypotheses – Experiment – Result, in solving the problems. It is important that we should think carefully about what these processes are.

There are number of ways of conceiving and categorising the science process skills. In this chapter the process skills as conceived by *Herlen (1998)*, which are assessed by Regional College of Education, NCERT, Mysore have been taken into consideration. The process skills identified are – observing, hypothesis, predicting, raising questions, investigating, interpreting, communicating, respect for evidence, flexibility and critical reflection.

1. *Observing:* Recognising the properties of objects and phenomena using the sense of sight, sound, taste, smell and touch is called observing. It helps in recollecting the properties of objects from previous experiences, identifying the objects, events and changes occurring in the environment. It provides an opportunity to distinguish objects on the basis of their properties and develops a habit of noting minute differences in the characteristics of objects and phenomena. Necessary and suitable opportunities and situations are to be provided to children to use their senses to explore objects and phenomena. Children may be allowed to discuss that all they have observed in a given context.
2. *Raising Questions:* Children are to be encouraged to raise questions, which can be investigable. Children should be allowed to ask any kind of question spontaneously. The teacher has to classify these questions into investigable and non-investigable questions.
3. *Hypothesis:* A hypothesis is an imagination consequent to scientific observation. Mostly children's hypotheses will be in the form of attempts to explain specific events in their experience rather than in terms of broad statements of principles, which explain a whole range of phenomena.
4. *Predicting:* Children often implicitly use patterns or hypotheses in making predictions. So teacher has to provide opportunities to make predictions in relation to patterns and hypotheses.
5. *Investigating:* This is a process of obtaining relevant data or evidence to verify hypothesis. While providing an opportunity to children to investigate, a teacher may have to assess how children are getting relevant data or evidence.
6. *Interpreting:* In order to develop an idea, children have to interpret what they found. They have to relate different kinds of information to each other. They should organise data efficiently, recognise the central themes/issues and assumptions, and compare trends and patterns of observed phenomenon. They should also inter-relationships between different phenomena; establish relationship between variables and from a habit of systematic inquiry. Sufficient time is to be provided, to children to interpret their findings.
7. *Communicating:* It is an ability to present or convey the

scientific information through different modes, such as, writing, speaking, drawing, etc.

8. *Respect for Evidence:* In the process of developing an idea, it is necessary that children should be willing to collect and use suitable evidences.
9. *Flexibility:* Willingness to change ideas in the light of available evidences is an important process skill. Hence, it is necessary to assess whether a child is able to change his idea when obtained evidences contradict the original idea.
10. *Critical Reflection:* A critical review of procedures executed is essential when evidences are in contradiction to the assumptions. It is then essential to assess whether a child is willing to review the procedures critically.

In order to develop science process skills in the students, the following factors should be kept in mind:

- Identify the content areas where a process skill can be exhibited.
- Prepare activities and materials to perform the skill.
- The activities may be both independent or integrated to content.
- Materials should be suitable and readily available.
- Situations and contexts should be identified and clearly stated.

**Impact of Science and Technology on Society**

If we look at ourselves and observe various activities we carryout from morning till night, we wonder that our life styles are completely different from that of our parents' times and our grand-parents' times. In this highly technical and materialistic world, our life styles are controlled by various components of science and technology in both urban and rural areas equally. The life styles of individuals have improved considerably and prominently only due to science and technology.

Science and technology has changed the man's way of life and his abilities to do work. It has also increased the rate of development of an area.

Some of the significant roles played by science in our daily life are:

1. *Science and Agriculture:* Food to store them properly and to supply them to various places is an important task. For fulfilling this task, new agricultural technology based on science has been developed. This resulted in the frequent and effective use of fertilisers and pesticides; advanced methods of.
2. *Science and Health:* Science has played a significant role in the field of medicine and health. The developments in science and technology have relieved the mankind from so many epidemics like smallpox, malaria and plague. So many medicines and vaccines have been developed for the mankind. Countless drugs and medicines are being synthesised in the laboratory. Scores of highly scientific and technical instruments have been developed, which are being used for accurate diagnosis, operation and even transplantation of organs. All these increased the life span of living things. Science forms the backbone for all these changes in living conditions.
3. *Science and Industry:* The discoveries of science accelerated the rate of growth of industries. Due to the drastic development of machines and instruments many of the activities are being done with less effort and energy. In this direction, so many instruments, machines and tools have come into day-to-day life to make life more easy and comfortable. For production and distribution of these machines in large scale to huge populations more industries are required. Science and technology have paved ways for the development of various industries all over the globe.
4. *Science and Living Conditions:* Science and technology have improved the living conditions of the human beings. All walks of life of human beings are influenced by the developments in science and technology. More facilities and instruments have been developed for a comfortable, healthy, safety and joyful living. Home conditions and various appliances have been developed. Now individuals can perform so many difficult tasks with ease or sometimes automatically which were impossible otherwise in the past. All these changes in the living conditions of people are due to the developments in science and technology.

5. *Science and Communication:* It is another important contribution of science. Communication has become a simple exercise due to the development of telecommunications, satellite technology, radio and television. Due to the recent Information Technology explosion and Internet accessibility the whole globe has become very small to know the various happenings and events. This has revolutionised the total global scenario of the world happenings. All the people can instantaneously watch every incident that happens on any part of the globe, under the earth and sea and in the space.
6. *Science and Vocations:* Due to the enormous amount of knowledge developed in science and technology, new jobs, vocations and professions have been identified and developed. New areas of work and working conditions have been provided. Millions of jobs are provided for those with science technical background.
7. *Science and Culture:* The life styles of individuals have been influenced a lot due to the developments in science and technology. So many orthodox traditions, customs and life styles have been modified in the light of science. These changes occurred in the ways of dressing, cooking, eating, living, behaving, organising, accepting, following and even thinking. All walks of life, now-a-days, are influenced by science. So many social orders and beliefs have been modified. All these things are due to the science and technology. Science has made a tremendous impact on the cultural life of the present society, which is a product of science. The thinking, feelings and actions of a modern man are practically guided by the effects of science. There is an involvement of science, direct or indirect, in all works and leisure of a modern man. Our customs and habits and feelings and attitudes have also been influenced by science.

## Science, Ideology and Society

Science, due to its highly structured nature has occupied an important place in the world of knowledge. Science has become a base for many subjects and a tool for the development of many. Science has created its own ideology i.e. the scientific philosophy, which is unique by its own. Science is universal in character and it has no barriers of any kind. It is international in outlook. The fruits of scientific discoveries of one country re enjoyed by the people all over the world. Science is neither concerned with caste, creed or colour nor recognises territorial barriers. Such a pattern, inherent in science ill definitely has an impact on the minds of the learners and in expected to develop broadmindedness in them. This attitude brings change in the minds of all the people of the society.

Science has made a tremendous impact on the cultural life of the present day society, which is a product of science. There is the involvement of science, directly or indirectly in all activities as we as leisure of a modern man. Our thinking, habits and attitudes have also been affected by science.

# 2

# History and Development of Science

### Introduction

In the previous chapter, you have studied about the meaning and structure of science, its scope and importance. You have also studied about the aims and values of teaching science before we go into the context of teaching you should knowhow this vast amount of scientific knowledge has developed. The nature of science can be observed right from its origin and throughout its development. Very few students might have studied the origin and development of science and the related information during their previous studies. In this chapter you are going to learn about the origin and development of science. You are also going to learn about the contributions of oriental and western sciences.

## HISTORY AND DEVELOPMENT OF SCIENCE

The origin of science can be traced back to the earliest times; its roots go down to the deepest strata of human history and to the darkness long before the beginning of human civilisation. The history of science, therefore, can be said to have begun with the history of human existence.

During the enormous stretch of time before the beginning of human civilisation, the early Homo sapiens (modern man regarded as a species) invented rudiments of practical rules of craft warranted by the necessities for their existence and survival. It is inferred that even during the period of Neanderthal man of post-primitive ages, some sort of stone equipment were used for hunting for food. History indicates that these Palaeolithic men of the Old Stone Age might have tried to make boats, houses and earthen pots apart from making use of crude stone arms for hunting. But the Neolithic men of the new Stone Age were comparatively more advanced; they knew agriculture and reared domestic animals, made houses and lived in groups. Thus, the early Homo sapiens probably discovered accidentally or through crude trial and error, such practical arts as fire making, cooking, pottery, weaving, building or use of metal for making arms. Such abilities imply 'observation of matter and events and an effort to use them for survival." These activities may be said to resemble science.

### (a) Early Science

By the middle of 4th millennium BC at least two written languages had appeared one in Mesopotamia and one in Egypt. It is also quite possible two others had aroused in India and China. As a result of their abilities to record observations, the early people discovered that the physical phenomena followed definite patterns from which they could predict future events. Babylonians believed that when a person was born his character was moulded by the constellation of stars in which the sun is placed. From this hypothesis, they developed the theory of astrology. They highly developed mathematics, multiplication tables and tables of squares and cubes. They created standards for measuring length, weight and time. Egyptians not believing in astrology did not develop their knowledge of astrology to the extent of Babylonians but had devised a calendar for 365 days. They were more interested in medicine and had remarkable intellectual activity in mathematics and engineering skills.

### (b) Greek Civilisation

Greek civilisation during 1500 BC is the Golden Age of Civilisation and is regarded by many as the highest level of mankind yet attained. Assuming that nature was understandable by man, Greeks cultivated many of the sciences and made their greatest contributions in the fields of astronomy, mathematics, botany, physics, structure of matter and medicine. They had a great love for abstract reasoning; Philosophy and Science were the same. They relied on observation and logic rather than experimentation.

### (c) Alexandrian Science and Dark Ages

In the fourth century BC, Alexander the Great in the city named after himself called Alexandria founded a great museum and an outstanding library in Egypt. It was scientific centre of the world between 300 BC and 400 AD. Great scientists like Pythagoras (BC 580-500), Hippocrates (BC 460-370), Aristotle (BC 384-322), Archimedes (BC 287-213), Euclid, Ptolemy (AD 90-168) etc. belong to the period.

Geocentric model of planetary system developed by Claudius Ptolemy based on the Aristotle's idea, which was not questioned for 1400 years and "Alchemy" an antecedent of chemistry originated during this period. In the fourth century AD, hordes of Barbarians from the north overran the Roman Empire destroying most of the intellectual activity on the European continent, which lasted for 600 years is known as the 'dark ages'. With the fall of Greek civilisation and the death of the philosophers and the scientists of Greece, a dark period prevailed upon the earth. The progress of civilisation, as if came to a temporary halt in Europe. Almost nothing significant could be added to the practical science that existed and there was complete intellectual stagnancy. The Christian church started building universities in Europe by 1000 AD to educate its leaders. Gradually intellectual centres developed at these Universities.

### *(d)* Birth of Modern Science

By the year 1600 AD people began considering nature as something to understand and a reformation in the sciences began. The Italian genius of fifteenth century, Leonardo da Vinci (1452-1519) gave great support to the new approaches to science through his drawings in anatomy and the biological and physical scientific objects. The first man to show the world the technique of understanding nature was the Italian genius Galileo Galilee (1564-1642) recognised as the founder of modern experimental science. A revival of science started in astronomy when he verified the heliocentric solar system suggested by the Polish Priest Nicolas Copernicus (1473-1543). Hence-forth, the experimental method was recognised as an effective means of investigation and was considered essential in the framing and testing of hypothesis for physical phenomena.

The period during the 17th and 18th centuries saw the development of scientific talent, which was instrumental leading us to the present position of living as a member of modern scientific society. The development of instruments of greater precision made measurements more meaningful. In the late 18th century, the development of analytical balance by Antoine Lavoisier and the development of atomic theory by John Dalton in 1802 placed chemistry on a firm basis. Later Mayer and Mendeleyev working independently classified all the known elements into families resulting in the present day periodic table. In 1895, the atomic age started in physics and chemistry with the two disciplines becoming more and more inter-related. In 1957, Russians put the first man made satellite 'Sputnik' into the orbit around the earth and began the space age.

**A Brief Introduction to Oriental and Western Sciences**

In spite of the achievements in various fields of science, even up to the nineteenth century, science did not find its place as a regular part of general education. Only the interested classes pursued science and lectures and discussions on science were organised by some universities and social agencies only in places where they had an audience interested in science but science as a part of general education goes back to the early medieval period in Western Europe.

**1. *Development of Science in Western Countries***

The first man of science to arouse interest in experimental science was Roger Bacon (1214-1294). He himself was a good scientist and delivered lectures on Aristotle's 'physics'. He emphasised the values of experimental studies in science over scholastic studies. The next three centuries saw the efforts of a series of notable persons of science, to popularise the study of science for its new practical outlook, in spite of the resistance from the orthodoxy of the church and the society, In 1543, De Revolutionibus Orbium Collestium an astronomical treatise by the Polish Astronomer Nicolas Copernicus was published and followed by the publication De Fabrica Corporis Humani of Vaselius. Their ideas heralded a new outlook challenging the older concepts of Ptolemy and Galan. The Italian genius Leonardo da Vince made science more realistic and vivid through his accurate drawings on anatomy and other mechanical aspects.

William Gilbert (1544-1603) of England tried to popularise science education in England. Francis Bacon (1561-1626) strongly advocated the method of experimentation and discovery in science. He emphasised the importance of teaching science and presented his scientific method in his celebrated work (1620). After the publication of Newton's Principia Mathematica in 1667, were some among the first to popularise education in Newtonian Physics.

In modern times, Herbert Spencer (1820-1903) tried to popularise education in science by declaring it as the most worthy of all knowledge. T.H. Huxley (1825-1885) strongly pleaded for the teaching of science for its disciplinary value, while Spencer advocated science as an instrument for physical and John Tyndall (1820-1893), a colleague of Faraday tried to popularise physics as a part of general education.

It is said that John Anderson was the first to start lectures on experimental physics in the 'Mechanics Institute', Glasgow, England in 1823 and Thomas Hall to start the first 'practical chemistry' in 1847 at the city of London School. Natural science was taught as an elective to language at Rugby. Later, however, physics was introduced there in 1837 and botany and chemistry in 1859. The report of Devonshire Commission of 1895 contains the details of the start of science teaching in the schools of England. Due to the introduction of science as a subject at the Oxford and Cambridge Universities of England, it encouraged the schools to include science as a teaching subject at the secondary level. This subsequently led to the introduction of different subjects of science in large number of secondary schools of England. H. E. Armstrong developed a method of teaching popularly known as "Heuristic Method." It must be admitted that the World War of 1914-1918 intensified the importance of 1944 included necessary provisions for wider science education in England. The advances of science and technology during twentieth century and the great scientific achievements on which the modern society has now become dependent, raise no question about its inclusion in today's school curriculum. In fact, science teaching has gained high priority in all the countries of the World.

**2. *Development of Science in India***

We think that science is modern and something recent. But our history also talks about our contributions to science and technology during the well-known Indus Valley Civilisation, which existed around 2500 BC. It is proved beyond doubt science and technology existed in ancient India. The ancient traditions of India reached great heights when the Vedic Aryans came to India around 1500 BC. The Rig Veda discusses the relationship that exists between the universe and the natural order.

Ancient India has made significant contributions to the world in the fields of mathematics, astronomy, agriculture, also to some extent in chemistry and medicine. But their progress could not develop beyond a limit.

The credit of development of number system goes to the Indians. The use of zero '0' is a revolution in Indian mathematics. There are so many famous mathematicians of ancient India who have contributed to astrology and mathematics. Some of the famous are Aryabhatta, Brahmagupta, Mahaveera, Varahamira and Bhaskara to name a few. In medicine we come across Dhanvanthari, Bharadwaja, Pathanjali, Charaka, Susrootha, etc. India's first satellite was named alter Aryabhatta, a great mathematician and astrologer. His book "Aryabhatiya" had laid foundations to Indian Astronomy. He developed the value of ? as 3.1419, tables of sine, distribution of time, theory of revolution of earth, astronomical constants, epicycles and positions of planets. The excavations at Harappa and Mohenjadaro reveal the well-planned constructions or towns, houses, water supply, drainage, preparation of bricks and earthen pots, handicrafts including garments. The Indian astronomers have developed luni-solar calendar based on the motion of the sun the moon. They identified various stars and given their names to the months. Vedas are mentioning about the concept of 'Permutations and Combinations'. The huge observatories at Delhi, Jaipur, Varanasi, Ujjain and Mathura erected by Sawai Maharaja Jai Singh called Jantar Mantar are famous monuments of Indian astronomy. He used the knowledge available from the observatory of Ulugh Beg at Samarkand of Islamic cultural background. Astronomy grew in India as a result of multi-cultural contributions.

Indians have studied the medicinal plants and their properties. In Susrutha Sanhita information regarding retina, hernia, caesarean, plastic surgery and surgical instruments is given and it described more than 300 different operations. In Charaka Sanhita methods of diagnosis of so many ailments including kidneys and skin etc., are mentioned. Charaka and Susrutha are not only experts in medicinal chemistry but they also mentioned about organic and inorganic elements. These treaties deal in detail with fundamental of pathology and anatomy.

In Rig-Veda a solar year has been divided into a calendar of 12 months each consisting of 30 days. Indians are successful in metallurgy based on Kanada's Atomic theory. Nagarjuna is an expert in chemistry and metallurgy. In his book 'Rasa Ratnakara', he explained about distillation, extraction, sublimation and the apparatus required for them.

In spite of all these and many contributions of Indians very few have been preserved and transmitted to the future generations in their full form. Even though the west admits the contributions of Indians to the world of science its position in the present day modern science is still foreign. There may be various reasons for this setback such as the Indian science and the history of its scientific and technological contributions are not well-recorded peculiar religion - cultural patterns and caste divisions in society, frequent invasions from outside, differentiation between intellectual and practical work in scientific pursuits.

**3. *Development of Science Teaching in India***

The modern system of education in India grew during the British period, which ultimately replaced the indigenous system of education that was in vague in India since ancient times. Initially, during the period of East India Company's rule and finally due to the combined efforts of the missionaries, government officers and enlightened Indians of the time, modern education slowly spread all over India.

The first efforts to introduce science as a school subject can be observed at Calcutta Madarasa (1780). Which had the provision for teaching of subjects to like natural sciences Quran, astrology, law, geometry, arithmetic, logic, etc? The subjects taught in Benaras Sanskrit Collage (started in 1791) included teaching of medical sciences.

Charles Grant who made disparaging remarks about Indian society was also a strong protagonist of modern education for the Indian people. He is often referred to as the Father of Modem Education in India. The Indian Government officially involved in the field of education with the Charter Act of 1813, which acted as the turning point in the History of Education in India. The minutes of Lord Macaulay of 1835 provided provision for utilisation of funds for imparting knowledge of English language and science through the medium of English language. During this period some English scientific books were translated into Indian languages and these helped the development of interest for education in science. The

Wood's education despatch of 1854 may be said to have laid the foundation for the present system emphasising European education. The report on Post-War Educational Development in India' of 1944 commonly known as the 'Sargent Report' envisaged two types of schools in India as Academic High Schools, which impart education in arts pure sciences, while the Technical High Schools will provide training in applied sciences, industrial and commercial subjects with intensive study of science. But in spite of all such reports and recommendations, science was not made a compulsory subject in the schools till very recently.

In the post-independence period the First Education Commission was the University Education Commission of 1948 under the chairmanship of Dr. Sarvepalli Radhakrishnan. This Commission made valuable recommendations in respect of secondary educations to include general science (Physics and Biology) as a course of study in secondary schools.

Later in 1953, the Secondary Education Commission under the chairmanship of Dr. Lakshmanaswamy Mudalir suggested the inclusion of General Science and Mathematics as compulsory core subjects at the middle as well as secondary level. The All India Seminar on Teaching Science held at Tara Devi, Shimla Hills, in 1956 (All India Council for Secondary Education) discussed all aspects of inclusion of General Science as a core subject for the secondary classes. This was the first agency in India to suggest acquisition with the training in "Scientific Method" and the development of "Scientific Attitude" as the aims of school science teaching.

In 1961, the Government of India constituted the "Indian Parliamentary and Scientific Committee" under the chairmanship of Sri Lal Bahadur Shastri, which studied the problems of science education in schools and made valuable recommendations. A committee on Plan Project was also set-up in 1962 to study problems relating to Science Laboratories in schools and the Science Apparatus and Equipment needs. In 1963, the USSR experts of UNESCO Planning Mission recommended on different issues on science education in secondary schools and suggested teaching science as a separate discipline at the middle stage and to lay emphasis on the practical application and activities which arouse interest, aptitude and ability in the subject. Subsequently, the NCERT (established in

1961) conducted pilot projects for evolving appropriate curriculum, textbooks and instructional material for teachers.

The Indian Education Commission (1964-1966) laid great importance to the teaching of science right from the primary to the university stage for development and prosperity of the nation and recommended upgrading school curriculum by research in curriculum development, revision of the textbooks and teaching learning material.

As a follow up of the Kothari Commission Report, the Ministry of Education and Social Welfare appointed an expert group to develop curriculum for the 10+2 pattern in 1973. The group drafted an approach paper in 1975. A publication entitled "Curriculum for Ten Year School – A Frame Work" was prepared by NCERT, which also prepared syllabic, textbooks and material in a phased manner.

These evoked a lot of criticism from parents, teachers and students. As a result of this a review committee under the chairmanship of Ishwarbhal Patel was appointed in 1977, which scrutinised the new syllabus and developed it keeping in view of the national goals of development and objectives of education.

The Government of India suggested some recommendations on Science Education through National Policy on Education (1986). According to this science should be considered as a core subject in the 10-year schooling. Situations from near environment should be used in teaching. Activities should be given a prominent place. Science education should cater for the development of investigativeness, creativity, questioning, aesthetic sense, appreciation and values in students. Students under non-formal modes should also be provided science education. Proper aims and objectives should be planned in order to achieve specific objectives and development of scientific attitude. In the year 2000 NCERT prepared a "Curriculum Framework for School Education – 2000."

We have now reached a stage when every citizen of India realises the importance of science learning. The impact of science and its achievements has made even a common man of today feel its need. People are now conscious to educate their children in a way so as to enable them to cope us with the personal and social problems obvious in a modem complex society due to the influence of scientific, technological and industrial progress.

**Brief Introduction to Aristotelian, Newtonian and Einsteinium Paradigms of Science**

The Greek period has produced great thinkers whose contributions are responsible for changing the entire course of world civilisation of later times. One the geniuses among a galaxy of contributors for scientific thought especially in mathematics and astronomy are Aristotle. He is considered as the father of Biology. He is a student of Plato. Aristotelian philosophy spread to the universities Western Europe and special emphasis was laid on the study of logic and mathematics. Aristotle's physics emphasised the values of experimental studies in science over scholastic studies. Based on the resources available at that time and his logical reasoning Aristotle suggested so many theories. Some of the ideas suggested by Aristotle were later found false by experiments conducted by Nicolas Copernicus, Galileo Galilee and Isaac Newton.

The father of modem science is Galileo Galilee. His experimental approach and method of verification has paved way for a new method of acquisition of knowledge. Newton's physics has the ingredients of this philosophy and approach. Newton has proposed so many theories and these attained the status of laws based on the universal verification and testing of the hypotheses. Newton's mathematical and experimental innovations have solved many mysteries of nature.

Albert Einstein was a great genius on this earth that left a permanent impact on his scientific work in the field of physics. For his contributions, he is known as the father of modern physics. His works on photoelectrons, Brownian motion, special theory of Relativity, mass-energy formula, photons, and general theory of relativity, which stunned the World, made him a world famous scientist. His approach mainly on theoretical calculations gave a new approach to the acquisition of new scientific knowledge.

**Life Histories and Contribution of Some Scientists in the Development of Science**

***A. Indian Scientists***

1. *Aryabhatta*

The first Indian built satellite launched by a soviet rocket in 1975 was in honour of Aryabhatta. This eminent Indian astronomical scientist and mathematician lived during 476-551 AD. Nothing is known about the parents of Aryabhatta who was very wise men, a great sage and a self-determined person. With his penance and mental concentration, it was possible for Aryabhatta to envisage the reality of the movements of planets.

It was believed in the early period of science that Aryabhatta lived in Patna of modern times (Pataliputra of Magadha kingdom of the past) near the famous Nalanda University, which encouraged the study of astronomy. But scholars now accept that he lived and worked in Kerala.

Aryabhatta's greatest work is "ARYABHATTEEYAM" which was written at his age of 23. Aryabhatteeyam is scholarly treatise on mathematics and astronomy in which has been introduced many new concepts extraction of a square and cube roots construction of trigonometric tables and eccentric epicentre models of a planetary notion. In other words, Aryabhateeyam is a literal work containing 4 quadruplets of 121 hymns. Out of these quadruplets contain discussions on the rotator and revolutionary processes of planets, determination of days and nights, movement directions of planets, determination of aeons, determination of weeks and months, sunrise, sunset, appearance of planets, comets, dooms day, period of different aeons discussions on all these aspects have been vividly explained in very lucid style by Aryabhatta. His major contribution to the field of astronomy and mathematics was the most accurate value of 'pi' as 3.1416 because 'pi' is the sign of the value of radius and perimeter of circle. In geometry, the use of 'pi' is very common. The earth is geoids body and it rotates on its own axis. Aryabhatta proved this fact and the other fact that the starts moved in an eastward direction with demonstration with illustrative examples. Till such time people believed that the earth was stationary object. Aryabhatta told the people that because of the earth's rotation, sunset and sunrise are caused and if one region of earth is in dark, the opposite region will have bright light.

In fact astronomy is a definite science dealing with the preparation of almanac, determination of the movements of sun and moon in the sky, knowledge of ellipses, new and full moons fixation of week's months etc. Astronomical science was known even during the 5th century, every much earlier to Aryabhatta. Only Aryabhatta around the 6th century developed astronomical science in to a regular science on a regular and systematic pattern. Only Aryabhatta brought algebra to light. He gave the word, complete details of capital amount of and the details of interest to be lived on the principal amount and also the necessary formula to be adopted in this aspect. Learned scholars have given keys to Aryabhateeyam, among who 'LATADEVA' is of importance as he happened to one of the students of Aryabhatta. Latadeva was highly learned astronomer.

To conclude, Aryabhatta continues to be a polestar for many more new investigations in astronomy, he was on authority on astronomy and his formulae in solving many astronomical problems are very simple and are accepted and adopted even today.

2. *Bhaskaracharya*

Among the Indian scientists we notice two kannadigas. One is Mahaveeracharya the Jain mathematics wizard and the second is Bhaskaracharya who is properly known as Bhaskara II, while Bhaskara was the disciple of famous astronomer Aryabhatta.

Bhaskara was a famous scientist also a poet of high calibre. He was born in present Bijapur in 1114 A.D. His father was a great learner mathematician known by the name Maheswarapadhyaya. Bhaskara's first teacher was his own father. When Bhaskara was only 36 years of age, he wrote a mammoth work entitled Sishanta Shiromani. This work is of 4 volumes and is a popularly known as Leelavathi or mathematics of Leelavati. The legend goes to say the reason for this nomenclature of the work. Though not much about his personal life, it is said that he had a son by name Lakshmidhara who was an intelligent mathematician. It is believed that Bhaskara had a daughter by name Leelavati from the mention made by this name is his famous work Ankaganita. Bhaskara learns from the horoscope of his daughter that she might become a widow after her marriage. With the parental comparison and responsibilities, Bhaskara thought of certain ways and means by which the state of widowhood may be warded off: he proceeded to select a proper Muhurtha for the marriage. But Lo! Where from could he get a watch to know the time to set the Muhurtha? Bhaskara invented his own Kalachakra. This clock was a hydro-wheeled vessel into which funnel was inserted and the container had to be with a certain amount of sand grains. The mechanism was set into operation at the time of sunrise and Bhaskara thought when the whole sand of grains get into vessel and drain out from the funnel the time for the marriage had to be fixed. But as Density had it, Leelavati, who was also gating the machine moved a bit way by which her nose stud skipped into the funnel and blocked the path for the sand grains to move down into the vessel below. By this time that was awaited for the marriage was an entirely different one and Leelavati's widowhood could not be warded half. In order to pacify his daughter and to keep her mentally engaged, it is believed that he taught her mathematics and he named the work after her name that had also assisted Bhaskara in his work.

'Leelavati Anita' of Bhaskara is a very vivid and simple work on Arithmetic, which would draw the attention of even beginner in arithmetic, an average student may even grasp it quickly. In bringing solutions to the intricate seems Bhaskara had made use of known materialistic items like the foresee swarm of beams, ponds, bird kingdom, forest fauna, bottle fields, pilgrim centres etc., as aids. The solutions are in the form of hymns, which can be learnt by the students to solve the problems. As for example if in a certain swarm of bees 1/5 of them buzz round the kalamba flowers 1/3 buzz round Shilindhra flowers, 3 portions of these numbers buzz round kutre flowers the remaining only one bee buzzes round the fragrant kethaka and malathi flowers, what is the number of bees. The solution is if the number of bees is presumed to be 'x' the answer must be 15 bees. Such sums and solutions are innumerable in this work of Bhaskara. This work has been translated to English by Kohi Brooke in 1817 AD, and to Parsee by Abdul Faz who was the minister to Akbar the Great. Many treatises have been published on this book.

Another equally interesting work of Bhaskara is Karnakuthuhala. This book, though on higher mathematics is more on certain calculations of astronomy. Thus Bhaskara wrote his first book on mathematics using the decimal system. Leelavati and Bijaganita filled in the gaps left out by earlier mathematicians. Bhaskara also introduced the mathematical signs 'minus' and 'plus'. He also noted that a division of an integer by zero would be equal to infinity.

After Bhaskara for nearly 700 years much work by mathematicians was not noticed. Absence or non-appearance of eminent men in this field of study and research could have been due to the foreign invasions made and battles fought. However,

Aryabhatta, Varahamihara and such other people of scientific eminence were the gifts offered to the world by India.

3. *Sir C.V. Raman*

Probably there is no one in the field of science who is not acquainted with the name of C.V. RAMAN. He was the first Indian Scientist to win the Nobel Prize for his famous discovery named after him as 'Raman Effect' in 1930. The most surprising thing is that he made this discovery with equipment worth hardly Rs. 200. Today, the Raman Effect is studied with the aid of equipment worth millions of Rupees.

Chandrasekhar Venkata Raman was born on 7th November, 1888, at Trichinopoli (now called Tiruchirapalli) in Tamilnadu. His father was a physics teacher in a college. Raman was an exceptionally brilliant student from the very beginning. When he passed his matriculation at the age of 12, his parents were keen to send him abroad for higher studies. But on medical grounds, a British surgeon advised them not to send him abroad. Therefore, Raman stayed in the country and was admitted in Presidency College, Madras. In 1904, he did his graduation and in 1907, he did his M. Sc. in Physics, and topped in the university. While he was a student in Presidency College he carried out many remarkable researches in the field of Physics. He worked on diffraction of light and his first research paper on this subject was published in 1906.

In 1907, after passing a Civil Service Competitive Examination, he became the Deputy Accountant General in Calcutta. Though he was very busy at this position, he used to spare his evenings for scientific research. He would spend his time after the office hours at the laboratory of the Indian Association for Cultivation of Sciences. Sometimes, he worked throughout the whole night. He got inspiration from Aushootosh Mukherjee who was the secretary of the Indian Science Association. He was so interested in the scientific research that in 1917 he resigned from his job and became the Professor of Physics at Calcutta University. During a sea voyage to Europe in 1921, he observed with wonder the blue colour of the Mediterranean and of glaciers. He became anxious to find out the reason of this blue colour. After returning to India, he did many experiments related to the scattering of light from water and transparent blocks of ice. On the basis of these experiments, he gave the scientific explanation for the blue colour of seawater and sky.

There is an interesting incident regarding the inspiration for the discovery of the Raman effect. On a December evening in 1927, Raman was showing a visitor some instruments in his laboratory. At that time, one of his young students, K.S. Krishnan, rushed to him and announced: "Professor Compton has won the Nobel Prize on scattering of X-rays." (He was the same K.S. Krishnan who later became the Director of the National Physical Laboratory, New Delhi.) Raman was equally delighted, but he was lost in some thoughts. He told Krishnan that if the Compton Effect was true for X- rays. It must be true for light too. He started experiments to verify his belief. He used monochromatic light from a mercury arc, which was passed through transparent materials, and was allowed to fall on a spectrograph to record its spectrum. In these experiments, he observed some new lines in the spectrum, which were later, called 'Raman Lines'. Four months later, on March 16, 1928, Raman announced his discovery of 'Raman Effect' to an assembly of scientists at Bangalore. For the discovery of 'Raman Effect' he won the Nobel Prize in Physics in 1930.

Many experiments have since been conducted throughout the World on 'Raman Effect'. It has been proved of utmost importance in understanding the molecular structure of chemical compounds. In fact, within a decade of its discovery, the structure of about 2000 compounds was studied. With the invention of the laser, the 'Raman Effect' has become a powerful tool for scientists. In 1924, Sir C.V. Raman was elected the Fellow of the Royal Society of London. He did a lot of work on magnetism and musical instruments. In 1943, he founded Raman Research Institute near Bangalore. Here he continued the scientific research till his death in 1970. His advice to young scientists was that scientific research needed independent thinking and hard work rather than sophisticated equipments. The apparatus used for the discovery of the Raman Effect did not cost him much.

Throughout his life, Sir C. V. Raman gave lectures on science in different universities and institutions. He was received everywhere with great honour. He never aspired for any high position. His ambition, instead, was to serve science.

4. *Subrahmanya Chandrasekhar*

Subrahmanya Chandrasekhar (1910-1995) was born in Lahore (then a part of British India) on the 19th October, 1910, as the first son and the third child of a family of four sons and six daughters. His father, Chandrasekhar Subrahmanya Ayyar, an officer in Governor Service in the Indian Audits and Account Department, was then in Lahore as the Deputy Auditor General of the North-western Railways. His mother, Sita (nee Balakrishnan) was woman of high intellectual attainments (she translated into Tamil, for example, *Henrik Ibsen's A Dolt House*), was passionately devoted to her children, and was intensely ambitious for them.

Subrahmanya Chandrasekhar's early education, till he was twelve, was at home by his parents and by private tuition. In 1918, his father was transferred to Madras where the family was permanently established at that time.

In Madras, he attended the Hindu High School, Triplicane, during the years 1922-25. His university education (1925-30) was at the Presidency College. He took his bachelor's degree, B.Sc. (Hon.) in Physics in June 1930. In July of that year, he was awarded a Government of India scholarship for graduate studies in Cambridge, England. In Cambridge, he became a research student under the supervision of Professor R. H. Fowler (who was also responsible for his admission to Trinity College). On the advice of Professor PAM Dirac, he spent the third of his three undergraduate years at the institute for Teoretisk Eysik in Copenhagen. He took his Ph.D. degree at Cambridge in the summer of 1933. In the following October, Dr. Subrahmanya Chandrasekhar was elected to a Prize Fellowship at Trinity College for the period 1933-37. During his Fellowship years at Trinity, he formed lasting friendships with several, including Sir Arthur Eddington and Professor E. A. Milne.

While on a short visit to Harvard University (in Cambridge, Massachusetts), at the invitation of the then Director, Dr. Harlow Shapley, during the winter months (January-March) of 1936, he was offered a position as a Research Associate at the University of Chicago by Dr. Otto Struve and President Robert Maynard Hutchins. Dr. Chandrasekhar joined the faculty of the University of Chicago in January 1937. And he has remained at this University ever since. Here Chandrasekhar theorised the physical process relevant to the structure and evolution of the stars. This theory is known as 'Chandrasekhar limit theory'. This limit imposes a restriction on the size of the highly dense star known as the 'white dwarf' which when exceeds the mass will explode to become a very bright stars called the 'supernova' and the matter will be shed in to the space which will be equal to the blast of thousands of atomic bomb. According to Astrophysicists the 'white dwarf stars are in Possession of the mass with in the limit of Chandrasekhar.' In 1935, Chandrasekhar worked on a 'Black holes' and had arrived at the speculation of their formation. A spoon full of these heavenly objects will weigh thousands of tones. This postulate of Chandrasekhar has not been accepted by other Astro-Physicists. He made significant contribution for understanding of the way matter and motion are distributed among the stars in a galaxy. He also worked on the atmosphere of stars.

During his last two years (1928-30) at the Presidency College in Madras, he formed a friendship with Lalitha Doraiswamy, one year his junior. This friendship matured; and they were married (in India) in September 1936 prior to his joining the University of Chicago. In the sharing of their lives during the past forty-seven years, Lalitha's patient understanding, support, and encouragement have been the central facts of his life. After the early preparatory years, his scientific work has followed a certain pattern motivated, principally, by a quest after perspectives. In practice, this quest has consisted in his choosing (after some trials and tribulations) a certain area, which appears amenable to cultivation and compatible with his taste, abilities and temperament. And when after some years of study, he felt that he has accumulated a sufficient body of knowledge and achieved a view of his own; he has the urge to present his point of view, in a coherent account with order form and structure.

There have been seven such periods in his life: stellar structure, including the Theory of White Dwarfs (1929-1939); stellar dynamics, including the Theory of Brownian Motion (1938-1943); the theory of radioactive transfer, including the theory of stellar atmospheres and the quantum theory of the negative ion of hydrogen and the theory of planetary atmospheres, including the theory of the illumination and the polarization of the Sunlit Sky (1943-1950); hydrodynamic and hydro magnetic stability, including the Theory of the Rayleigh-Bernard Convection (1952-1961); the equilibrium and the stability of ellipsoidal figures of equilibrium, partly in collaboration with Norman R. Lebovitz (1961-1968); the general Theory of Relativity and Relativistic Astrophysics (1962-1971); and the Mathematical Theory of Black Holes (1974-1983). His students Chem Ning Yang and Tsung-Dao Lee have been awarded Nobel Prize even before him in 1957. Dr. Chandrasekhar died in his house in U.S. at the age of eighty-five on 25 August, 1995.

### B. *Western Scientists*

#### 1. *Nicolas Copernicus*

Copernicus, as he is popularly known as was a polish astronomer was postulated in 1507 that the sun and not the earth was a centre of the universe, with the earth and other planets revolving around the sun and the stars in the vast and limitless haven surroundings then all. He said that the earth revolves on its own axis to cause days and nights and this accounted for the old belief that the earth was at the centre of the universe. This theory is known as the Copernicus world system, which is found in his famous book, entitled on the revolution of planets, which was published on the day of his death, which occurred during 1543. The finding of Copernicus was often a long period of constant and careful study. Though Copernicus was not the first man state this truth. People did not accept it. He could not therefore publish what he found and this fact on the planetary system was made known the world only by Galileo.

Copernicus was born on the 19th February, 1473 in Totun, Poland of wealthy merchant who was also a magistrate and civic leader. Copernicus was very intelligent and after the premature demise of his father, with the guidance and benevolence of his uncle, he began to study at Cracow at the age of 17. There he studied mainly philosophy, astronomy, geometry and geography, during the time of Copernicus, astronomy was of greater importance for a general study and there was a great need for setting up an accurate calendar for proper celebrations of the church holidays, Copernicus also studied medicine for the useful service in the church where his uncle was a bishop. At the age of 39, his uncle died and Copernicus had to work as a canon of the cathedral in the church at Franeesbug.

Copernicus became famous for his mathematical and philosophical formulations of the theory of the universe. Also being at the service of the people in the church Copernicus published a book on his findings and observations entitled 'Revolutions'.

Copernicus' De revolutionibus orbium coelestium, published a few days after his death, gave new currency to the ancient

Pythagorean hypothesis that the Sun was at the centre of the universe and that the planets (including the Earth) revolved around the Sun.

2. *Galilei Galilee*

Galilei was born on February 15, 1564 in Pisa (Italy), the son of Vincenzo Galilei, well-known for his studies of music, and Giulia Ammannati. He studied at Pisa, where he later held the chair in mathematics from 1589-1592. He was then appointed to the chair of mathematics at the University of Padua, where he remained until 1610. During these years he carried out studies and experiments in mechanics, and also built a thermoscope. He devised and constructed a geometrical and military compass, and wrote a handbook, which describes how to use this instrument. In 1594, he obtained the patent for a machine to raise water levels. He invented the microscope, and built a telescope with which he made celestial observations, the most spectacular of which was his discovery of the satellites of Jupiter. In 1610, he was nominated the foremost Mathematician of the University of Pisa and given the title of mathematician to the Grand Duke of Tuscany. He studied Saturn and observed the phases of Venus. In 1611, he went to Rome. He became a member of the Academia dei Lincei and observed the sunspots. In 1612, he began to encounter serious opposition to his theory of the motion of the earth that he taught after Copernicus. In 1614, Father Tommaso Caccini denounced the opinions of Galileo on the motion of the Earth from the pulpit of Santa Maria Novella, judging them to be erroneous. Galileo therefore went to Rome, where he defended himself against charges that had been made against him but in 1616, he was admonished by Cardinal Bellarmino and told that he could not defend Copernican Astronomy because it went against the doctrine of the Church. In 1622, he wrote the saqqiatore (The Assayef), which was approved and published in 1623. In 1630, he returned to Rome to obtain the right to publish his Dialogue on the two chief world systems, which was eventually published in Florence in 1632. In October of 1632, the Holy Office to Rome summoned him. The tribunal passed a sentence condemning him and compelled Galileo to solemnly abjure his theory. He was sent to exile in Siena and finally, in December of 1633, he was allowed to retire to his villa in Arcetri, the Gioiello. His health condition was steadily declining — by 1638, he was completely blind, and also by now bereft of the support of his daughter, Sister Maria Celeste, who died in 1634.

Galileo died in Arcetri on 8 January 1642. For the family of Galileo, within the Museo Sala IV is entirely dedicated to Galileo and his studies; among other things are preserved the lenses, the inclined plane, the lodestone, and the model of the application of the pendulum to the clock, several portraits and a relic.

■ *Galileo Galilee – Mechanics*

The story of Galileo and Leaning Tower of Pisa is well-known in the history of science. At the age of 23, when he was working as a lecturer in Mathematics in Pisa University, he read in a religious book that if two bodies of different weights were allowed to fall simultaneously from the same height, the heavy body would hit the ground first. In fact, this was a statement made by Aristotle. Galileo was the first man who proved this statement wrong. For this he selected the 180 feet high leaning tower of Pisa. On the demonstration day, Galileo went up to the seventh floor of Pisa Tower with two metals baits weighing 100 pounds and 1 pound respectively. Thousands of people had turned up to witness his experiment. Among the crowd were many professors and students of Pisa University. Many superstitious spectators had blind faith in Aristotle's statement given thousands of years earlier. They were freely abusing Galileo. Galileo put both the balls on one edge of the roof very carefully. Some people among the crowd became curious, but most spectators were whispering with each other that this man would prove to be a fool very soon by his own experiment. Galileo dropped both the balls simultaneously. The people were wonders truck when the two balls hit the ground at the same time. In this way, many years old superstition was proved wrong scientifically. People may differ about the truth of this story. However, it is true that Galileo could understand many facts about gravitation and that is why he could prove the truth by his experiment.

■ *Galileo Galilee – Astronomy*

In the early years of the seventeenth century Galileo adapted a telescope for the viewing of extremely small objects. Between 1619 and 1624, he began to produce microscopes or "occhialini" as he called them. The Galilean microscope is made up of the tube of a telescope, of reduced size, furnished with two lenses. Galileo gave his "occhialini" to various people. He sent a letter to Federiqo Cesi accompanying the instrument, in which he explained the means by which it was focussed and the arrangement of objects for observation. Galileo fabricated the first telescope. He has written in one of his books that when the news of his telescope reached Venice, the king Sing Aroia called him. The whole court was surprised to see this instrument. Many people went up to the top of the Venice Church and saw the ships nearly 10 times nearer with the help of this instrument. For about a month many people tested his telescope. With this instrument Galileo later explored the universe. With his telescope, he saw the satellites of Jupiter. He also proved that our Milky Way is composed of millions of stars.

■ *Galileo Galilee – Thermometry*

Galileo dedicated himself to research on heat at the end of the 16th century. The invention of the thermoscope seems, then, to belong to his Paduan period. This device was used to carryout experiments on the relationship between changes of temperature and variations of the level of the liquid. The work of the Accademia del Cimento, which led to the birth of the Florentine thermometer, had its origins in Galileo's early research.

■ *Galileo Galilee – Magnetism*

Between 1600 and 1609 Galileo devoted himself to studying magnetism, inspired by William Gilbert's de Magnete. He attempted to increase the strength of loadstones by means of special armatures. Galileo gave one of these to Grand Duke Ferdinand II.

3. *Antoine Laurent Lavoisier*

Antoine Laurent Lavoisier was a prominent French chemist and leading figure in the 18th-century chemical revolution, which developed an experimentally based theory of the chemical reactivity of Oxygen, co-authored the modern system for naming chemical substances. He has also served as a leading financier and public administrator before the French Revolution.

Lavoisier, Antoine Laurent, a French chemist and physicist was born in Paris in 1743. He belonged to a family of lawyers. Though he studied law, he did not take up the profession. Lavoisier was much inclined towards the different branches of science. He perfected the results of many a scientific findings. To finance his investigations, he took up the job of farmer-general of taxes, and from here followed string of jobs, making his presence felt in every field that he ventured in. He was systematic in his experiments as much as he was concerned about experiments as much as he was concerned people's welfare. He brought about and implemented peoples welfare. He brought about and implemented several reforms in the hospitals and prisons, leaving his imprint also on the political arena.

His remarkable contribution in chemistry through the nomenclature for chemicals attributed to him was a great success. He put an end to the ancient myth which compared life to 'a flame that blazes and is then extinguished', was no longer a simple metaphor but a scientific reality. The other feathers to his cap are introducing a universal measuring system as also the decimal system. Thus, Lavoisier's contributions are varied. He had a number of works and books to his credit. His colleague, Joseph Louis Lagrange, commented when Lavoisier was tried for misappropriation of funds and was finally condemned to the guillotine, in 1894. "It took them only an instant to cut off that head, but it is unlikely that a hundred years will suffice to produce a similar one."

The year 1760 was a sorrowful one for Antoine as he lost his sister Marie at 15. But the intellect and the praise gained by Antoine at school was the only redeeming factor for his family, which was consoling the loss of Marie. Antoine became the sole passion for the family to look forward to in the absence of his sister. However, he left the college in 1761, without his graduation honours. On the advice of his father, he started studying Law, graduated in 1764 and began practice at the Parlement de Paris. Lavoisier's interest in this profession did not last long, but was indebted to it for his precise language, which became his forte. While in secondary school he was introduced to meteorology and science in which he was to later prove his intellect. He was also exposed to different disciplines in science, like botany, anatomy, electricity, mineralogy and geology. Lavoisier mastered all these sciences having acquired proficiency in alt these subjects with an open mind and childlike curiosity. His legal knowledge enabled him to reason on/or about anything or everything that came his way. Lavoisier attended the Mazarin College from 1754 to 1761 studying chemistry, astronomy, botany and mathematics. His first publication in chemistry appeared in 1764. His writings though formal, had an easy flow and were pleasant to read, because of its clarity and precision. His demonstrations were presented in a perfectly logical and didactic way. He took great care to present his discoveries with exactitude.

Lavoisier had keen interest in geology too. He carried out a series of tests on mineral water and observed the work of miners and metallurgists. He discovered that there was a connection between geography, demography and economic activity. His vast readings made him formulate a theory on the boundaries of the sea and the arrangement of the continents. Lavoisier also specialized in meteorology. At 20, he had begun to note down barometric and atmospheric parameters and continued this activity throughout his life. The experiments carried out by using the prevalent thermometers did not satisfy him, so he formulated precise rules for the fabrication and graduation of thermometers.

In 1788, he showed that air is a mixture of gases, which he called oxygen and nitrogen. He disproved the Phlogiston Theory and demonstrated that oxygen is required for combustion, rusting, and respiration. His interest in chemistry and zoology inspired him to write the pioneering work on 'Anatomy and Physiology'.

Lavoisier earned out a series of tests on mineral water and observed the work of miners and metallurgists, all of which would nourish his reflections as a chemist. At the same time, he discovered the connection between geography, demography and economic activity. He assumed that a cyclical movement of ebb and flow of the ocean had deposited a succession of sedimentary layers on the earth to measure the thickness, altitude and extension of each of these geological stratums, Lavoisier attempted to establish barometric contour lines. But the technique proved to be insufficiently precise and it was through geodesic observations carried out with the protractor quarter circle developed by Jean Charles de Borda that he would subsequently check his data.

Meteorology was his specialty. The barometric observations obtained by using Reamur thermometer were not satisfying, so for the fabrication and graduation of thermometers, he deposited 12 standard models at the Academy of Sciences, in 1781, studying natural electricity and the formation of thunder, he demonstrated with Laplace and Volta that hydrogen, nitric acid, carbon dioxide and water vapour, in passing from the liquid to the vapour state emitted electrical charges measurable by the electrometer. In association with Benjamin Franklin, he installed lightning rods on the roof of St. Paul's church.

A Swiss scientist Bengt Ferner attributed the steady lowering of the levels of the oceans, to a transformation of water into earth. Lavoisier attacked this myth of transmutation of water into earth. He boiled water for 100 days in a 'pelican', a glass recipient whose shape resembles the bird's form, and demonstrated that the residue obtained was not due to transmutation of water, but rather to the dissolving of the pelican's inner surface in the water. He carried out this demonstration by applying for the first time what would become the basis of his scientific method of the weighing of the elements of reaction, thanks to the use of precise scales.

4. *Michael Faraday*

Today, thousands of power stations all over the world are providing electricity with the help of generators. Without the invention of the generator electric power could not have been a reality and moreover it is difficult to visualize out life today without electricity. The credit of inventing this machine goes to Michael Faraday. When he made the first generator he was not aware that his invention would turn out to be one of the most important boons of the scientific age.

Michael Faraday, the father of Electromagnetic induction, was born in 1791 a Newington, England. He was the son of a blacksmith and worked as an apprentice in book binding during his early years. He developed interest in science after he attended some lectures given by Sir Humphrey Davy in 1813. He began to work as Davy's assistant at the Royal Institution. One year later, he accompanied Davy on a European tour. This turned out to be a highly rewarding experience for the modestly educated young scientist.

After his return to Royal Institution, Faraday had to work hard, since he was the main source of income for the Institution, which was then facing financial problems. During this period, Faraday worked in the field of glass and steel. He performed many chemical analyses and investigated the chlorides of carbon for Davy. His work resulted in the discovery of benzene in 1825. Davy left the Royal Institution, but Faraday was immensely influenced by Davy and carried out many experiments for him. When Faraday discovered in 1823 that gases could be liquified by pressure, Davy got the credit. After this, serious differences crept in between the two, so much so that Davy opposed the election of Faraday as a Fellow of the Royal Institution.

On 1820, Hans Oersted discovered that when electric current passes through a conductor it could produce magnetic field. Faraday heard about this and thought that it would also work the other way round that is, magnetic field can generate electricity. He carried out experiments; he invented the process of electromagnetic induction. He demonstrated that if a magnet is moved inside a wire loop, electricity is generated. He also demonstrated that if a current carrying wire is suspended near a magnet it revolves around the magnet. These experiments made him famous throughout Europe. In 1831, he made the first dynamo. Joseph Henry also made a generator at the same time. All modern dynamos, generators and transformers are based on the work of Faraday and Henry.

One famous incident of Faraday's life is worth mentioning. When he invented electromagnetic induction, he presented an experiment to demonstrate it before many people who came from all over the world. Among the spectators was a lady with her young baby. Faraday took a coil of copper wire and connected its ends to a galvanometer. He inserted a bar magnet into the coil. With the insertion of the magnet the needle of galvanometer moved, indicating generation of electricity. When he removed the magnet, the needle moved back. Faraday explained to the audience that this was basis of generating electricity. When the demonstration was over, the lady became angry. "Is it an experiment? Have you called the people to fool them?" she asked Faraday. Faraday replied politely, "Madam, just as your child is quite young, so is the case with my experiment. So far it is like a baby. In future, it may be of utmost importance." Faraday's statements have come true today. There is no electric generator and transformer, which do not work on the principle of electromagnetic induction. If Faraday had not invented electromagnetic induction, perhaps we would have not got electricity.

In the next few years, Faraday demonstrated by passing currents through solutions that all kinds of electricity however generated, was the same. In this way, he developed the laws of electrolysis in 1834, which are taught to the students of physics even today. In 1839, Faraday suffered a mental breakdown, his convalescence took four years. His breakdown left him with a poor memory, which grew worse with time. However, he returned to his work and started investigating the effect of a magnetic field on non-metallic substances. He discovered paramagnetism and diamagnetism. Although Faraday was very fond of giving lectures on science subjects, in the late 1850s he had given it up because of his failing memory.

In 1861, Faraday, then 70 retired from the Royal Institution and moved to a house in Hampton Court that Queen Victoria has offered him. By now his condition was so bad that he required permanent assistance. On 25 August, 1867, he breathed his last. He was given a private funeral at High Gate Cemetery, Faraday was a scientist noted for blending theory and experiment in his researches. He had little money to spend on apparatus and knew no mathematics. Many of his inventions were not put to use until decades after his death. Two electrical units are named after Faraday. One is the Faraday Unit used in measuring quantities of electricity, and the other is the Faraday Unit used in measuring the capacity of capacitor.

# 3

# Aims and Values of Teaching Science

## Introduction

In the previous chapter, you have studied about the definitions, meaning and structure of science. After going through the structure of science it is important for a teacher to learn the aims and values of science. This information helps you to know the purpose of teaching science and the things to be borne in mind while teaching science. In this chapter you are going to learn about the aims and values of science.

## AIMS OF TEACHING SCIENCE

The aims of teaching any school subject must always be directed towards achieving the aims of education in general. Various definitions of the term 'aim' finally lead to a general conclusion that education must develop to the full, the potentialities of the individual learner in accordance with the general good of the society. The teaching of science as a subject, must therefore, contribute to the all-round development of the child so that he comes out as a socially useful and efficient citizen of the modern scientific would. This aim is, however, too general and too broad to be meaningful in the classroom situation. The broad aims should serve as a frame of reference and should be regarded as directions of growth.

Various commissions, committees and organisations have suggested various aims in different ways. They can be summarised under the following categories:

### Acquisition of Knowledge and Information

The students studying science should acquire knowledge of scientific facts. Principles and events of nature. The knowledge of science will help the learner to live an intelligent and efficient life in a modern society. Such knowledge must be appropriate to the age, stage and ability of the learners. Knowledge of science should make the learner to understand, adjust and if necessary change his immediate environment as required. The teacher must teach science to fulfil the need of 'knowledge for the sake of knowledge'.

**Development of Favourable Habits**

The teacher should see that desirable need for learning science is instilled in the learners' minds and that such qualities are reflected in their everyday habits. Science is a pursuit of truth and its pursuit demands intellectual honesty, diligence, perseverance, tenacity, patience, concentration of mind, unbiased judgment and objective observation. These qualities also help the learners to become self-confident. Further, studies of science should develop healthy habits. The teacher should also inform them about health and hygiene as well as public sanitation and emphasise their application in everyday life. The students should form the habit of taking care of personal health and community sanitation.

**Development of Interest and Appreciation**

Science study without interest will not be meaningful and permanent. The science teaching should stimulate interest in the learners in the subject. They must develop interest to pursue scientific activities within and outside the school, read scientific news and literature, organise science clubs and exhibitions and try to apply scientific knowledge in everyday activities. The students studying science should be able to appreciate the contributions of science for the well-being and comfort of mankind and how the ideas and achievements in science have contributed to the progress of human civilisation. They should be able to realise the tremendous progress of experimental science, the marvels and wonders of modern science and the application of science to every field of human activity. The teachers in their process of teaching should lead the learners to see the impact of science on society and to feel their responsibility as members of the modern society.

**Training in Scientific Method**

Through teaching of science, the students should be trained in scientific method or procedure while solving scientific problems. It involves logical steps in the process, which is derived from the application of critical thinking and systematic procedure.

**Development of Scientific Attitude**

This is an important component of aims of science teaching. The have to make efforts to point out these aspects in the process of teaching of science and try to inculcate this outlook in the behaviour pattern of the learners.

**Development of Skills and Abilities**

The teaching of science should aim at developing in the learners various skills involved in the study of science. Such as skills in drawing diagrams sketches of specimens, apparatus, constructional skills, experimental skills for arranging and organising experiment, handling instruments and apparatus, observation skills and skill of solving problems. The study of science should develop the ability to identify a problem, analyse and interpret a problem ability to improvise apparatus, generalise and predict results and also the ability to locate the source of information. They should also develop abilities to express and discuss on scientific problems and the ability to organise science clubs and fairs.

**Science Studies form the Basis of Future Career**

The teacher should be able to select students to enable them to pursue scientific discipline of science at higher level.

**Provision for Utilisation of Leisure**

Science provides a host of technical and intellectual activities, which they provide fruitful engagements for leisure time. The pupils should be encouraged to prepare simple useful material, articles and their maintenance and also for the preparation of charts, models, etc., and improvisation of different instruments.

## VALUES OF TEACHING SCIENCE AS A SUBJECT

Galilei Galileo (1564-1642) once said that in questions of science, "The authority of a thousand is not worth the humble reasoning of a single individual." Though he referred to the faculty of theoretical reasoning, he was the first experimental scientist. While learning science, the learner develops certain faculties through reasoning and experimentation, which no other subject can provide.

The rapid advancement of science and technology and increasing need for scientists and technologists have made it all the more important to provide for science based education in the schools. Vigorous methods for the cultivation and promotion of science should be adopted. The Secondary Education Commission has recommended that every secondary school pupil should study general science as a compulsory subject, so that he gains a basic quantum of scientific knowledge as a part of his general education.

Science, as a teaching subject, possesses the various values as any other subject for which it is included in the curriculum as a teaching subject such as intellectual values, utilitarian values, cultural values, moral values and aesthetic values etc. But in addition, the study of science inculcates certain other disciplinary values peculiar to it, which cannot be provided through other subjects. Besides these, the teaching of science imparts training in the 'Scientific Method' and develops 'Scientific Attitude', which are very valuable and at the same time are transferable to other situations in life.

Science has now become a compulsory subject in the school curriculum because of its multifarious values to the individual as well as the society.

**Intellectual Value**

Science is the most inexhaustible storehouse of knowledge. It is opening new horizons of knowledge everyday and is continuously adding to the cultural heritage of mankind and ever-increasing new knowledge, new explorations and new ideas. It makes man aware of the vastness of the unknowable knowledge in the universe. The fundamental characteristic of science is its possibility of unlimited growth. Science as a subject offers the widest range of knowledge to the learners. Acquiring knowledge for the sake of knowledge itself is one of the characteristics of civilisation. Science is both the foundation as well as the structure of our modern civilisation. The intellectual value of science stresses the fact 'knowledge for the sake of knowledge'. It gratifies the intellectual universe we live in. The study of science gives us a real insight of ourselves and the things around us. Science has its own discipline. It sharpens our intellect and makes us intellectually honest and develops critical observation and reasoning. It teaches to arrive at conclusions without any emotional bias or prejudice.

**Utilitarian Value**

It is hardly necessary to elaborate the utilitarian or practical values of science. We are living in a world of science and technology. Every thing or every event happing around us demands some knowledge of simple scientific facts or principles. Science has entered in our life and daily activities so much that our existence would become impossible without it. The achievements and benefits of science touched all sectors and all levels of the modern society. The modern man has applied science and technology for the well-being of the mankind by inventing machines and by harnessing the resources of nature. The recent advances in the fields of science and technology and the wide application of the achievements of science in industry, agriculture, medicine, transport, communication, information technology, space and their use for making life comfortable and raising the standard of living justify the utilitarian value of science.

**Vocational Value**

The study of science has opened innumerable avenues for pursuing different vocations. A student of science can study engineering, medicine, agriculture or any similar subject and make his career in that profession. In addition, scientific activities have given rise to many varieties of crafts and allied services. Science, therefore, gives opportunities for career making and pursuing professions and vocations. Its study in school forms the basis for many useful hobbies and other productive activities in the later life of the students. It offers a wide variety of opportunities in industries as technicians, scientists and research workers in new fields of science.

**Cultural Value**

Science has played an important role in determining the culture and civilisation of a country from time-to-time. It has a direct influence in dispelling many traditional beliefs and orthodox customs a consequence of new techniques of science, the social organisations have also changed, which gradually bring about corresponding political and social change. Culture, in addition to knowledge, includes all activities, thoughts, feelings, and patterns of individual or social life of men. The study of science gives opportunity for the development of favourable traits of human character, which become a positive contribution to the cultural life of the society.

**Moral Value**

Science is an activity where truthfulness is the most essential condition for success, where success is not possible on any other terms. Science is truthful because it has practically no temptation to be anything else. In his work the scientific man has superb moral standard, but the value of his example to the rest of mankind is limited by the fact that in his work, the scientist is not a perfect man—he is only a seeker of truth. The study of science brings behavioural change in the learner and enriches his character and personality. Science gives opportunity for creative thinking and constructive imagination. Further, science is a subject where ideas can be experimented upon and verified. The learner develops the habits of searching for the truth. These qualities affect the pattern of behaviour of the learner.

**Aesthetic Value**

At higher levels, art and science are not different. There can be no good piece of art without the application of science and on the other hand, there is artistic or aesthetic element in all the scientific activities. The great thinkers have always been stressing the unity of science and arts and those they originate from the same root. The whole charm of science lies in its aesthetic aspect. To a man of science practical application in just a by-product of his autonomous activity. The scientist feels an intrinsic charm in revealing the harmony of nature. Nature exhibits an order, which is governed by general laws that we can understand. Had nature not possessed a harmony that was beautiful to contemplate, science would not have been pursuing. In nature everywhere, we come across what Einstein calls 'pre-established harmonies', which is beautiful and the discovery of such harmonies is the concern of science. So there is compromise between the artist and the man of science or in other words science and art are basically the same.

**Training in Scientific Method**

The study of science trains the students in attacking the problem according to a certain definite and distinct procedure, which we may call as the scientific method. This training, which he receives in studying science, can be applied to solve other problems arising in new situations. In brief scientific method involves the following steps:

(*a*) Defining the problem
(*b*) Analysing the problem
(*c*) Collecting the data
(*d*) Interpreting the data
(*e*) Formulation of tentative solutions or hypotheses
(*f*) Selecting and testing the most likely hypotheses
(*g*) Drawing conclusions and making generalisations
(*h*) Application of generalisations to new situations.

**Development of Scientific Attitude**

The study of science brings development in the behaviour. For instance, science is an interest-awakening subject; its pursuit demands persistent efforts, diligence and patience. Any experimentation in science requires keen observation, concentration of mind as well as accurate presentation of facts. There is no place for prejudice or bias in science. Hence, it requires critical and objective observation; logical and impartial judgment intellectual honesty, perseverance, concentration of mind, broadmindedness, persistence, accuracy of measurement, patience, respects for others opinion and truth. These qualities of mind if cultivated through the teaching of science will be carried over to manifest the general behaviour of the learner. This will prove useful for living as an efficient social individual in the society. The biographies of scientists incorporated in the science course develop a scientific attitude among the learners. The description of the scientists' pursuits, their tenacity and perseverance are worth reading. Such a study brings out the scientists' attitude towards science and their hopes and frustrations on their way to discovery.

Along with the above values science provides means for utilisation of leisure. Scientific activities provide the best hobbies and pastimes for worthy utilisation of leisure. The learning of science also develops problem-solving skills. If properly cultivated through the teaching of science, the students can apply this skill to solve problems in his personal or social life.

# 4
# Objectives of Teaching Physical Sciences

## Introduction

The aims are, however, too general and too broad to be meaningful in the classroom situation. The broad aims should serve a frame of reference and should be regarded as directions for growth. It is therefore necessarily to formulate objectives to serve as roads towards attainment of the ultimate ends, aims. These objectives should be such that the learner's growth and development are directed towards their relation and they are practically attainable through the teaching of the subject. Therefore, suitable objectives of teaching the subject should be selected. In this lesson you are going to learn about the definition of objectives, their importance to teaching of science and the purpose of classification to the teacher. You are also going to learn about the taxonomy of educational objectives developed by Benjamin S. Bloom and the objectives from various domains.

## Meaning and Importance of Objectives

### *Definition of Objectives*

"What kind of abilities and skills should be developed in the students? This is a question frequently developed in the minds of the teachers and they think vigorously to get a suitable answer to it. The answer to the above question may be in the form of a statement called objectives. It is neither simple nor uniform to state objectives. We can successfully focus our attention on the product, i.e., the pupils' behaviour at the end of the course, and state it in terms of his knowledge, understanding, skill, application, attitude, interests, appreciation, etc., but these goals should be in accordance with the aims of teaching the subject, science.

The school programme even though only a part of the total educational programme – it is an important one. It can achieve only a part of these aims – objectives. Hence, 'Objective is a point or an end view of the possible achievement in terms of what a student is able to do'. Objective is a part and parcel of an aim. It is a narrower term. Aim is a very broad term.

## Objectives Originate from Aims

| *Aims* | *Objectives* |
|---|---|
| 1. Aims are directions in education. Education cannot progress in a desirable direction without aims | 1. It's a point showing the possible achievement |
| 2. Achievement of aim is beyond the of school programme | 2. It's an end view of the possible achievement |
| 3. Aims are directions given to entire educational system within and without | 3. It is the objectives that can be achieved |
| 4. Aims take a long time to be achieved | 4. Objectives may be changed from subject to subject |
| 5. Aims fail to help in selecting appropriate content | 5. Objectives are realized in stages |
| 6. These are meaningless to teachers. | 6. Content can be selected and they help in day -to-day activities meaningful to teachers. |

### *Educational Objectives*

Educational objective – is a statement of expected results. It is not a wish or a hope, but what students should be able to do at the end of the period, which they could not do before.

1. It states the way in which your students will be different as a result of your teaching.
2. It states the way to handle knowledge and mental processes used.
3. It states what the student would be able to do.
4. It is a statement of why you want your student to learn.
5. It states what you are trying to accomplish.

## Objective

An objective is a point or an end – view of the possible achievement in terms of what a student is to be able to do when the whole educational system is directed towards the educational aims.

### *Importance of Objectives*

1. An aim is a direction in education. Education can't progress in a desirable direction without aims.
2. An objective on the other hand is a point showing the possible achievement in that direction i.e. an end view of the achievement. Therefore, objective gives direction to education. They tell the classroom teachers in which way to go, a decision that is of paramount importance before the first step is taken on an educational journey.
3. It is the objective that can be achieved and not the aims, which are beyond the scope of school system or school programme.
4. Aims of education can't be changed from subject to subject while objectives may be changed from subject to subject.
5. Objectives originate from aims.
6. Attainment of each objective takes us one stop forward in the achievement of an educational aim. If objectives are realized by stages, an educational aim may be achieved one-day.
7. Aims are broad and hence can't help in selection of content and methodology but objectives do so and also help a teacher in his day-to-day activities.
8. Speedily, objectives help the teacher in instructional planning, guide student's learning and provide a criterion for evaluating their learning outcome.
9. Objectives aid in evaluation, which again helps us to refine objectives.
10. Persons concerned with education are more likely to have a clear idea of what the out comes of education ought to be.

## Bloom's Taxonomy of Instructional Objectives

### *Purpose of Taxonomy of Educational Objectives*

1. To establish the accuracy of communication regarding the objectives of education.

2. To reduce the vagueness arising out of such loosely defined terms and concepts as 'to know, 'to reason', "understanding", "interest, etc., and to understand the relationship among them.
3. To become a means of more precise communication system in the field of education.
4. To establish a common understanding about a hierarchical classification of objectives.
5. To become a means of understanding the sequence and organization of human development.
6. To be a great help in clearly defining and meaningfully evaluating the educational standards of a school.

### *Taxonomy of Educational Objectives*

An attempt was made to build a taxonomy or classification of educational objectives. Dr. Benjamin S. Bloom of Chicago University introduced the idea of classification of educational objectives. He classified the educational objectives into three main areas or domains. They are:

1. Cognitive Domain.
2. Affective Domain.
3. Psychomotor Domain.

1. *Cognitive Domain* is concerned with the ability to do a task.
2. *Affective Domain* is concerned with the will or desire or attitude to do the task. Hence, Cognitive and Affective domains are theoretical aspects of human behaviour.
3. *Psychomotor Domain* is concerned with the practical aspect.

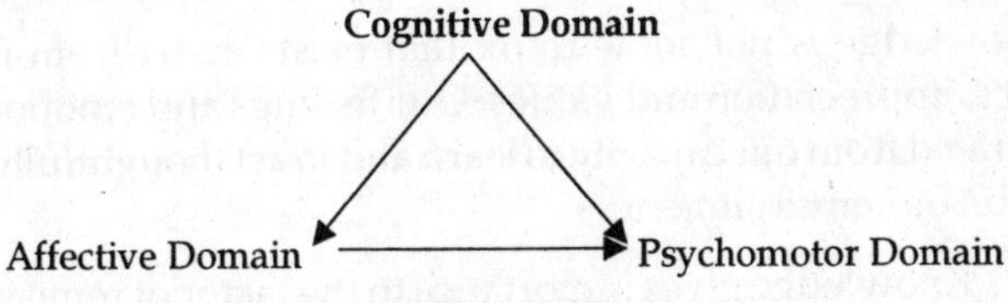


**Instructional Objectives**

| *Cognitive Domain* | *Affective Domain* | *Psychomotor Domain* |
|---|---|---|
| (The recall or recognition of knowledge and the development of intellectual skills) | (Changes in interests and values and the development of appreciation and attitudes) | (Development of manipulative or abilities and skills) |

## Cognitive Domain (Benjamin S. Bloom, 1956)

This domain includes those objectives which deal with recall and recognition of knowledge and development of intellectual abilities and skills (mental or intellectual abilities involved in perception, knowing and abstract thinking) includes objectives which deal with thinking, knowing and problem solving.

Cognitive taxonomy contains six major classes of objectives arranged in a hierarchical order on the basis of complexity of task and arranged from simple to complex behaviour and from concrete to abstract behaviour.

### Knowledge

It involves the recall or recognition of specifics and universal, methods and processes of a pattern, structure or setting. It is defined as remembering of previously learned material. This may involve the recall of a wide range of material from specific facts to complex theories, but all that the required is the bringing to the mind appropriate information. Knowledge represents the lowest level of learning outcomes in the cognitive domain.

The cognitive domain includes objectives, which deal with thinking, knowing and problem solving. It includes those objectives, which deal with the recall or recognition of knowledge and the development of intellectual abilities and skills.

Dewey – "knowledge is not merely a state of consciousness but consists of what we consciously do or make use of understanding what is happening in straightening out a perplexity by conceiving the connection between ourselves and the world in which we live."

Knowledge is not some think that exists apart from interest, attitudes, appreciation and values. Our feelings and emotions can't be separated from our capacity to learn and to act thoughtfully within and upon our environment:

- Knowledge gives importance to the factor of remembrance power related to behaviour,
- This remembrance may happen by recognizing objects or processes, or
- The pupil feeds some information into his mind and stores in it. After some time according to his behaviour he shows remembering this information.

- It is natural that some changes may occur in the information stored – but they are minimum,
- Knowledge is abstract and universal – this knowledge is separated, processed, characterized, specified, arranged definite format in various permutations and combinations and judged at various higher levels of metal process, and
- The objective knowledge is differentiated from other objectives of cognitive domain in a specific context. In this, a mental process of remembering.

  Plays an important role, in others it is only a part.

1. *Knowledge of Specifics*
   - Specific or undifferentiated or indivisible body of knowledge.
   - These are fundamental in venous subjects – These are elements of that branch.
2. *Knowledge of Technology*
   - Knowledge of specific verbal and non-verbal symbols.
   - Defining technical terms by giving their attributes, properties or relation.
   - Familiarity with vocabulary of ditto rent fiesta, geometric figures.
3. *Knowledge of Specific Facts*
   - Knowledge of dates, years, persons, events, places, sources of knowledge, etc.
4. Knowledge of ways of mere of dealing with specific organizations, studying, judging criticizing ideas and phenomena.
5. *Knowledge of Conventions*
   - Characteristic ways of dealing writ and presenting ideas and phenomena.
   - The traditional symbols, social behaviour, styles, rules used commonly dithionate, separation of maps, etc.
6. *Knowledge of Trends and Sequences*
   - Knowledge of processes, directions, movement of phenomena with respect to time.
   - The effect of information technology in the culture and international relations of a country.

7. *Knowledge of Classification and Categories*
   - Classification of classes, sets, divisions, etc., for the benefit of fundamental of a given subject, told or problem – various types of locomotion.
8. *Knowledge of Criteria*
   - For testing and judging facts, principles, opinions and conduct.
   - Knowledge of criteria for judging the nutritive value of foods.
9. *Knowledge of Methodology*
   - Knowledge or methodology or technique or procedure used in specific fields or specific problem-solving or enquiry.
10. *Knowledge of Universals and Abstractions*
    - Knowledge of major ideas, schemes and patterns by which, concepts and ideas are organized.
    - Highest level of abstentions and complexity.
11. *Knowledge of Principles and Generalizations*
    - Briefing of observations of phenomena into abstract statements.
    - Recognizing or racotocting a generalized statement or principle.
12. *Knowledge of Theories and Structures*
    - Includes the body of principles and generalizations together with their intimidation which present a clear rounded and systematic view of a complex phenomena promoter field.

**Comprehension**

It represents the lowest level of understanding and includes translation, interpretation and extrapolation. It is the ability to grasp the meaning of the material. This may be shown by translating information from one form to another (words to numbers of symbols or vice versa) by interpreting (explaining or summarizing) and extrapolating (establishing future trends by predicting consequences of effects). These learning outcomes go one step beyond the simple remembering of information and represent the lowest level of understanding.

**Application**

The use of abstractions in particular and concrete situations is called application. This refers to the ability to use learned material in new and concrete situation. This may include the application of such things as rules, methods, concepts, principles, laws and theories. Learning out comes in this area require a higher level of understanding than those under comprehension.

**Analysis**

The ability to breakdown a communication or material into its component parts so that its organizational structure may be understood or the relative hierarchy of ideas is made clear and/or the relations between the ideas expressed are made explicit. This includes the analysis of elements, analysis of relationships and analysis of organizational principles.

- The intellectual of analysis are in a higher order than in comprehension and application.
- Analysis breaks down and information into its constituent parts.
- If finds out the interrelation between each part and the way they are organized to form a whole.
- The ultimate aim of analysis is to find out the construction of an organization but it is a base for a comprehensive understanding and evaluation.

It is impossible to draw a separating line between comprehension, application or analysis.

1. *Analysis of Elements*
   - Any information is a combination of different constituent elements.
   - Ability to identity the unclear assumption and identifying but from assumed theories.
2. *Analysis of Relationships*
   - After identifying the various elements, the interrelationships between various elements are analyzed.
3. *Analysis of Organization and Principles*
   - It is very complex to analyse the construction and organization.

- It analysis the internal construction.

**Synthesis**

Refers to the ability to put parts together to form a new whole. This may involve the production of a unique communication (theme speech) a plan of operation (research proposal) a set of abstract relations (schemes for classifying information). Learning outcomes this area stress creative behaviour with major emphasis on the formulation of new patterns of structures.

- Synthesis is joining together various elements to form a new whole.
- It is combining various elements of a body which is either not clear. or
- Partially correct to provide a complete structure.
- It synthesis a new body combining new material with old experiences.
- Production of a unique communication.
- Production of a plan or proposed set of operations.
- Derivation of a set of abstract relations.

Evaluation is concerned with the ability to judge the value of material information (statement, novel, poem, report, etc.) for a given purpose. The judgments are to be based on definite criteria. Their may be internal criteria (organization) or external criteria (relevance to the purpose) and the student may determine the criteria. Learning outcomes in this are the highest in the cognitive domain since they contain elements of all of the other categories, plus conscious value judgments based on clearly defined criteria. Evaluation aims at making judgments about the value, ideas, works, solutions, methods and material etc.

- Value judgment about a process, method, object, solution, etc.
- Judgment in terms of internal evidence.
- Judgment in terms of external criteria.

**Affective Domain (David Kratwohl, Benjamin S. Bloom and Masia, 1964)**

This domain includes objectives of interests, attitude, values and development of appreciation and adjustment. Objectives under this domain are not stated very precisely and clearly. It is difficult to describe behaviour under this domain since internal feelings and emotions are not as clear as over behaviour manifestations. Testing procedures for this domain are not still standardized and they are hard to define and evaluate. Affective domain is divided into five major classes arranged in a hierarchical order on the basis of the level of involvement.

### Receiving

Receiving is to orient the learner to learn. That is the first step that he is willing to learn what is being given to him. This category has three different levels:

- *Awareness:* The pupil to aware of a scientific activity in the school.
- *Willingness:* The pupil is willing to take part in the scientific activity.
- *Attend (controlled or selected attention):* The pupil attends the activities arranged by the science club.

### Responding

This level crone after the learner has given his attention. This includes behaviours it compliance and willingness to respond and getting with Mautton by responding. This stage includes reading about the subject and enjoying in various extracurricular activities or projects.

- *Responds:* The pupil responds to the questions asked by the teacher.
- *Willingness to Respond:* The pupil raises hands to the answer questions.
- *Satisfaction by Responding:* The pupil obtains satisfaction joy by responding.

### Valuing

This is an abstract concept, which is an importance element of behaviour. This is not motivated by desire to comply or obey but he is motivated because of his own valuing or assessment and commitment (to certain ideas and values). This proceeds in three stages:

- Acceptance of a value.
- Preference of a value.
- Commitment to certain point of view.

### Organization

Organization pertains to the building of a system of values. A value is conceptualized in the abstract and the conflicts between the values are resolved and inter-relationships are established. This involves the cognitive behaviours of analysis and synthesis. The maturity level required for this level is beyond that attained in the beginning years of formal education.

### Conceptualization

When the learner develops certain values, he encounters situations for which more than one value is relevant.

### Organization

In such cases, he is able to organize the values in to a system.

### Characterization

This is the highest level of affective domain and includes characterization of a person's behaviour by certain controlling values, ideas or beliefs and the integration of values and attitudes into a world view or total philosophy of life. The individual acts constantly in accordance with the values he has developed.

- Affective domain is the realm of feelings, emotions and attitudes in people as distinct from the cognitive domain.
- Students often gain support in the learning situation when their positive feelings and attitudes can be summoned as motivation.
- Some educationists lay greater stress on cognitive objectives and poorer job in evaluating affective objectives.
- Another reason why affective behaviour is under–evaluated in school is that it is very difficult to change it or to measure it accurately.
- The techniques of attitude change are not nearly so well-developed or as successful as the techniques for attaining cognitive objectives.
- Measurement in the affective domain is difficult because.

1. Lack of behavioural objectives.
2. Educators do not fry to evaluate whether or not affective objectives have been attained.

**Psychomotor Domain (Simpson, 1966 and Kibler *et al.*, 1970)**

This domain refers to the conscious control of muscular movement as in the psychomotor development of infants. It includes those objectives that deal with manual and motor skills.

This proposed taxonomy is based on the concept of coordination between various muscular actions. Behaviour, which includes muscular action and requires neuro-muscular coordination, is grouped under this domain.

***Imitation***

Imitation of an action or performance.

***Manipulation***

Manipulation of an action. This includes differentiating among various movements and selecting the proper one.

***Precision***

Precision is reproducing a given act. This includes accuracy in proportion and performance and exactness in performance.

***Articulation***

Articulation among different acts. This includes coordination, sequence and harmony among acts.

***Naturalization***

Here an individual's skill attains its highest level of proficiency in performing an act with the least expenditure of psychic energy. The act becomes so automatic that is attended to unconsciously.

**Specific or Behavioural Objectives – Learning Experiences**

***How to State Objectives***

- The behavioural objective the one that specifies what the learner will be doing when we evaluate.
- The behavioural objectives use action verb, whereas non-behavioural objectives do not.
- Behavioural objectives tend to be more specific than non-behavioural ones and that is why behavioural objectives are known as specific objective of specifications.

**Criteria for Writing Statements of Objectives**

1. As the term non-behavioural objective suggests, the statement of an objective should contain a non-action verb.
2. The statement of objective should indicate a worthwhile objective.
3. The statement of objective should be related to the human ability which can be developed or achieved with the help of education.
4. The statement should also mention the subject-matter area (content) through which a particular ability is to be developed.
5. The statement of objective should be the torn of students achievements and not in the form of the teacher's intention.
6. The statement of objective should be written in the form of the achievement of every single student and not in the form of the achievement of a group of students. This will persuade the teacher to pay individual attention to his students.
7. The statement of objectives should contain only one of ability to be developed or achieved or modified.

**Instructional Objectives**

***Objectives from Cognitive Domain***

1. *Knowledge:* The pupil acquires knowledge of__________

   ______________________________________________

2. Understanding the pupil develops an understanding of

   ______________________________________________

3. *Application:* The pupil applies his knowledge and understanding of new and unfamiliar situations______

   ______________________________________________

***Objective from Psychomotor Domain***

4. *Interest:* The pupil develops skill in ______________ through the study of______________________________

***Objectives from Affective Domain***

5. *Interest:* The pupil develops skill in ______________ through the study of______________________________
6. *Attitude:* The pupil develops a positive attitude through the study of______________________________________

7. *Appreciation:* The pupil develops an appreciation of____ ________________________________________

## Specifications and Elarning Outcomes

The objectives stated earlier are too vague for the teacher, as they do not offer an adequate and enough direction to the teacher. As a result, the teacher cannot prepare and organize appropriate learning activities for his pupils. Hence, there is a need for specifications. These should be specific and must be expressed in behavioural terms. The term "specifications" is synonymous with "specific objectives or behavioural objectives". The statement of a specification contains an action verb. A good rule-of-thumb is writing to ask you: "Can my students do these things?"

For example, a class teacher gets the following answers to the above question. My pupil

1. explains the working of Vernier Callipers.
2. changes Fahrenheit temperature to Cesisius.
3. labels the parts of sensitive balance.
4. discriminates among various types of lenses.

## Specifications or Behavioural Objectives

What occurs as a result of learning experience is termed as the learning outcome; while a stated desirable outcome before the students undergo learning experience is termed as specification.

With specifications phrased or expressed in the right manner, the teacher knows:

(*a*) What to teach (content–teaching points);
(*b*) How to teach (learning activities to be organized); and
(*c*) What the pupil is to be tested for (evaluation procedure).

For example in the statement – the pupil draws a thermometer, neatly and accurately – the statement serves a double purpose.

On the one hand, it states a desirable outcome before the students undergo a learning experience. On the other hand, the statement states what behavioural change one would observe as a result of the learning experience.

This means that the statement shows a specification and a learning outcome. The statements of specifications or learning outcomes may run into hundreds, but with the help of taxonomies, one may classify them under a relatively small number of headings.

**Criteria for Writing the Statement of Specifications**

1. The statement of specification should contain an action verb.
   *For example:* The pupil solves the given problem on specific density:
   'To solve', 'to compare', 'to describe' and 'to explain', etc. are action verbs. The statement should be in the form of an over activity or behavioural outcome, which is observable and measurable. This ultimately increases objectivity in evaluation. The statement should indicate clearly the behaviour as an expected outcome so that the teacher can organize his learning activities accordingly, which may prove more effective, fruitful and meaningful.

2. The statement of specification should contain two parts:
   (*a*) The *modification* part, which includes the pupil's expected behaviour, and
   (*b*) The *content* part, which includes the subject-matter area, i.e., content through which behaviour is to be changed or modified.
   *For example*: The pupil explains the causes of an earthquake.
3. The statement of specification should indicate a worthwhile specification.
4. The statement of specification should be in the form of the student's achievement and not in the form of the teacher's intentions.
5. The statement of specification should be written in the form of the achievement of every single student and not in the form of the achievement of a group of students.
6. The statement of specification should contain only one behaviour to be developed or achieved or modified.

Although there are certain techniques of working objectives in order to make them behavioural, the major problem in writing arises out of the fact that teachers have not clearly spelt out for themselves the behaviours which are reasonable indicants of their non-behaviourally stated objectives. To write objectives that can be reasonably evaluated requires considerable knowledge about:

(*a*) the subject-matter that is taught; and

(*b*) about the change in behaviour one hopes to bring about among students as a result of an instructional sequence.

It is certainly more difficult to work objectives behaviourally in some areas than in others. Whenever an objective is from the affective domain, it is particularly difficult to specify it behaviourally.

The stating and writing of objectives is two – step process:

1. We should state the instructional objectives as general learning outcomes. For these statements, no – action verbs such as "understands", "applies", etc. are permissible.
2. We should list under each instructional objective a representative sample of the specific types of explicit behaviour which indicates the attainment of the objective, i.e. that which describes the terminal behaviour which pupils are to demonstrate when they have achieved the objective.

As a partial help for teachers, who recognize the need for behavioural objectives a list of action verbs are given below.

**List of Functional, Behavioural, Action Verbs**

| Defines | Describes | Identifies | Labels | Outlines | Reproduces |
|---|---|---|---|---|---|
| Selects | Detects | Suggests | Adapts | Represents | |
| States | Lists | Converts | Defends | Infers | Distinguishes |
| Estimates | Explains | Extends | Generalizes | Gives | Examples |
| Paraphrases | Predicts | Rewrites | Changes | Computes | |
| Prepares | Produces | Relates | Shows | Solves | |
| Uses | Breaks | Down | Differentiates | | |
| Illustrates | Points out | Separates | Subdivides | | |
| Categories | Combines | Compiles | Composes | Generates | Files/Revises |
| Writers | Appraises | Concludes | Contrasts | Criticizes | |
| Justifies | Discriminates | Recognizes | Applies | Assigns | |
| Diagnoses | Interprets | Etc. | | | |

**Instructional Objectives and Specifications**

**1. *Knowledge***

The pupil acquires the knowledge of scientific terms, facts, concepts, processes, phenomena, techniques, theories, principles, etc.

*Specifications*

- The pupil recalls the scientific terms, facts concepts, processes, phenomena, techniques, theories, principles, etc.
- The pupil recognizes the scientific terms facts concepts, processes, phenomena, techniques, theories, principles, instruments, devises, etc.

**2. *Understanding***

The pupil develops an understanding of scientific terms, facts, concepts, processes, phenomena, techniques, theories, principles, etc.

*Specifications*

- The pupil distinguishes the relationship between related concepts.
- The pupil classifies the items as per criteria.
- The pupil generalizes the observed phenomena.
- The pupil translates symbolic statements into verbal statements and vice versa.
- The pupil detects errors in faulty statements, concepts, processes, etc.
- The pupil rectifies errors in a given statement, arrangement, formula, etc.
- The pupil explains a given principle, process or a statement in his/her own words.
- The pupil cites illustrations and examples.
- The pupil selects appropriate tools, apparatus, etc.
- The pupil discriminates between closely related concepts, principles, processes, etc.
- The pupil compares and contrasts the physical phenomena, concepts, principles, etc.

**3. *Application***

The pupil applies his knowledge and understanding of scientific terms, facts, concepts, processes, phenomena, techniques, theories, principles, etc. to new and unfamiliar situations.

*Specifications*

- The pupil analyses an example, a problem or a situation.
- The pupil formulates a hypothesis.
- The pupil collects relevant data about a hypothesis.
- The pupil judges the adequacy of the data.
- The pupil infers or predicts from the data.
- The pupil suggests theories, procedures, illustrations, improvisations, etc.
- The pupil interprets the given chart, graph, table, data, etc.
- The pupil solves the problems.
- The pupil adapts the himself with new instruments.
- The pupil gives scientific reasons.
- The pupil represents the relationships between quantities graphically.
- The pupil applies the theories and principles to daily life situations.

**4.** ***Skill***

The pupil develops skills in practical skills like observation, performance, recording and setting up of physical science experiments.

*Specifications*

- The pupil takes measurements and reads instruments accurately.
- The pupil checks tools, apparatus, chemicals, etc.
- The pupil sets up appropriate apparatus and tools for experiments.
- The pupil cleans apparatus and tools before and after the experiment.
- The pupil takes precautions in handling the apparatus and doing the experiments.
- The pupil records the list of materials, procedures, observations and generalizations.
- The pupil performs experiments with reasonable speed and accuracy with neatness.

- The pupil replaces the old apparatus or instruments or methods by new ones.
- The pupil sketches diagrams neatly.
- The pupil draws graphs.
- The pupil calculates the results.
- The pupil carries out simple and original projects.

5. *Interest*

The pupil develops interest in scientific and natural phenomena and work and their application in day-to-day life i.e., in the world of science.

*Specifications*

- The pupil reads on his own scientific literature and biographies of scientists.
- The pupil on his own visits places of scientific interest and importance.
- The pupil participates in scientific activities like science talks, science debates, science projects, etc.
- The pupil on his own collects specimens and materials.
- The pupil contributes on his own exhibits concerning scientific matter for a display.
- The pupil on his own writes articles.
- The pupil on his own takes up hobbies of scientific interest.
- The pupil on his own meets scientists whenever possible.

6. *Attitudes*

The pupil develops scientific attitude through the study of physical sciences.

*Specifications*

- The pupil respects research findings contrary to the existing theory.
- The pupil accepts only those suggestions based on conclusions derived from scientific research.
- The pupil expresses his ideas with concrete examples and support.
- The pupil records and interprets his observations honestly.
- The pupil arrives at judgments after weighing all possible evidences.

- The pupil considers new ideas and discoveries and inventions free from prejudice.
- The pupil is unbiased in his approach to problems.
- The pupil admits his mistakes unhesitatingly.
- The pupil cooperates with others while working in the laboratory or field.
- The pupil follows the guidelines and instructions issued by such international organizations life UN, UNESCO and UNICEF etc.

7. *Appreciation*

The pupil appreciates the contribution of physical sciences to all fields of knowledge and to human life and welfare.

- The pupil realizes the importance of physical sciences in human progress.
- The pupil express his/her joy, excitement and thrill at every new discovery in physics and chemistry.
- The pupil shows respect and admiration to scientists.
- The pupil derives pleasure in understanding the advancements of science and technology.
- The pupil manifests a spirit of scientific enquiry.

# 5

# Methods of Teaching Physical Sciences

## Grouping of Teaching Methods

I. D. Zyrev suggested the use of knowledge and skills as the basis of classification of methods resting on word (narration), object (image), and action (motion). In this scheme, three corresponding classifications of methods are oral, observation and practical. Let us now classify the common teaching methods.

1. *Oral Methods:* Lecture and Historical methods.
2. *Observation Methods:* Lecture—demonstration, Observation method.
3. *Practical Methods:* Heuristic, Project, Problem solving, Laboratory method etc.

The other commonly used basis of classification is based on the level of activity of students or teachers i.e. if the student is active, the method is called student centered and where the students are mere passive participants and teacher is active, the method becomes teacher centered.

- *Teacher Centered Methods*—Lecture, Lecture-Demonst-ration, and Historical.
- *Student Centered Methods*—Heuristic, Project, Laboratory and Problem solving.

The teacher centered methods use traditional instruction where the teacher lectures, uses the textbook, and promotes discussion. The student centered instruction is non-traditional instruction where the students work independently and in groups on specific assignments. They discuss lessons in the text by focusing upon "real world" applications. The teacher uses visuals, field trips, guest speakers, and current events to teach the lessons. The role of the teacher is to monitor the students and give advice or ideas so that they may draw conclusions and solutions independently or cooperatively. Hands on learning are another technique that constitutes a non traditional approach. The "hands-on" curriculum centers on experiments, group activities, and real life applications. Real life applications of subject-matter focus upon why students need to learn what they are learning. Schools where hands-on teaching and learning are the order of the day tend to be a little noisier, a little more active than traditional schools. Schools that teach the hands-on approach are more likely to be using an integrated curriculum. A thematic, integrated curriculum is where several teachers share the role as facilitator with students in a particular unit.

## LECTURE METHOD

The lecture is one of the oldest and basic methods of teaching. Although experience and educational researches have shown that the lecture is less effective than activity methods at school level, we find that most science teachers spend nearly 50 per cent or more of their time lecture. The use of lecturing depends on the subject-matter, teaching philosophy of teacher and overall learning situation. Formal lecturing is used largely to build up basic theoretical knowledge, which must be gained before practice of skills. If the number of students in a class is large, teaching resources are scarce or time available is limited, lecturing appears to be the only way out.

### Definition

Carter Good defined lecture as "An instruction procedure by which the lecturer seeks to create interest to influence, stimulate or mould opinion, to promote activity, to impart information, or to develop critical thinking, largely by the use of the verbal message, with a minimum of class participation; illustrations, maps, charts or other visual aids may be employed to supplement the oral technique."

### Steps in a Lecture Method

We are all aware that the three main stages in any educational activity are Planning, Presentation and Evaluation and Conclusion.

We shall now see what the steps are under these heads in the lecture method.

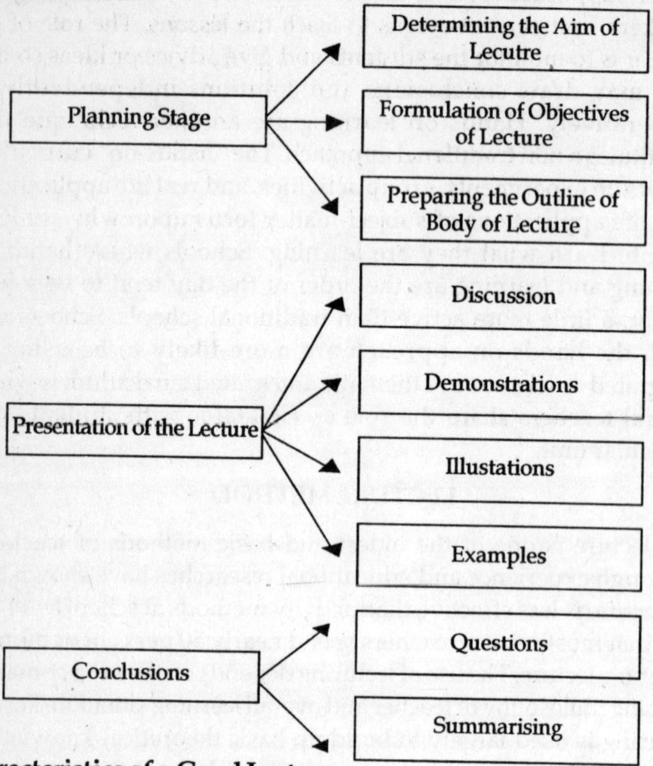


**Characteristics of a Good Lecture**

An enthusiastic presenter is one who is well-organised, challenging and clear in his presentation.

- The presentation includes an overview, logical organisation and closure.
- The organisation of the lecture should be explicit to the audience so that they understand the relationship between various parts.
- Use of verbal clues and visual aids enhance the lecture.
- Attention and motivation is sustained through use of anecdotes, physical activity, humour etc.
- The audience is challenged to become intellectually involved with the topic being presented.
- Keeping these characteristics in mind we shall now be able

to judge the quality of any lecture we attend to in future. Isn't it?

*Advantages of Lecture Method*

Think of the advantages of lecture method. Now see if it matches our list given below:

1. The lecture method is the most economical way of getting a large amount of information to a large class. A teacher can convey the information in a minimum time, thus enabling the syllabus to be covered within a stimulated time. It is economical in terms of money and time.
2. The lecture is useful in imparting factual information in an efficient manner to convey facts to students who have difficulty in following their texts.
3. The lecture helps to channels the thinking of students in a given direction.
4. Some abstract topics in science are best taught by the lecture method. The teacher through tact, style and presentation can get his/her message through effectively.

*Limitations of Lecture Method*

We shall now list some of the main limitations of the lecture method.

1. Science as we all know is more than a body of knowledge. Hence mere pouring in of information is psychologically unsound and leads to neglect of development of skills.
2. Science is best learnt by 'doing'. There is no provision for activities in this method as students are passive listeners.
3. The method doesn't cater to individual grasping capacities of students. The rate of imparting information by a teacher may be too fast for some who become restless and inattentive. For some others it may too slow leading to boredom.
4. A poorly planned, poorly delivered lecture fails to motivate the student.
5. Lecture method doesn't cater to the affective and psychomotor domains.
6. Teacher needs a lot of prior knowledge to prepare a lecture.

*Application of Lecture Method*

1. Despite all the criticism levelled against it, lecture method is widely used even today. It is accepted that the method is

not applicable to teach science at especially lower classes. In higher levels it can be used for following purpose.

2. Starting or introducing a new and difficult topic.
3. Explaining certain difficult and theoretical points, which cannot be demonstrated?
4. Explaining a demonstration.
5. In summarising and recapitulating certain generalisations and scientific principles at the end of a lesson.

## LECTURE DEMONSTRATION METHOD

As the name indicates the method includes the merits of lecture method and demonstration method. The teacher performs an experiment and goes on explaining what the teacher does. It takes into account the active participation of the students and is thus not a lop-sided process like lecture-method. The students see the actual apparatus and operations and help the teacher in demonstrating the experiment and thereby they feel interested in learning. It is difficult to talk about things the students have to imagine. It is easy for students to understand and remember concrete things. This method works on the principle "Concrete - Abstract". The students observe the demonstration critically and try to draw inferences. Thus the students develop their power of observation and reasoning. Further, lecture demonstration method helps us to minimise the limitations in lecture method. Unlike lecture method it takes co-operation of students and they don't remain passive spectators.

This method serves two purposes:

1. To provide means of making certain parts of subject-matter clear by objectifying it.
2. To do the above with as much economy possible. It is useful for children of all ages as for it provides concrete experiences along with verbal ideas, which has desirable effects upon the students.

### Steps in a Lecture—Demonstration Method

Do you remember we had diagrammatically represented the steps in a lecture method? Why don't you try to do so for the lecture demonstration method also?

We shall represent the steps in using this method diagrammatically.

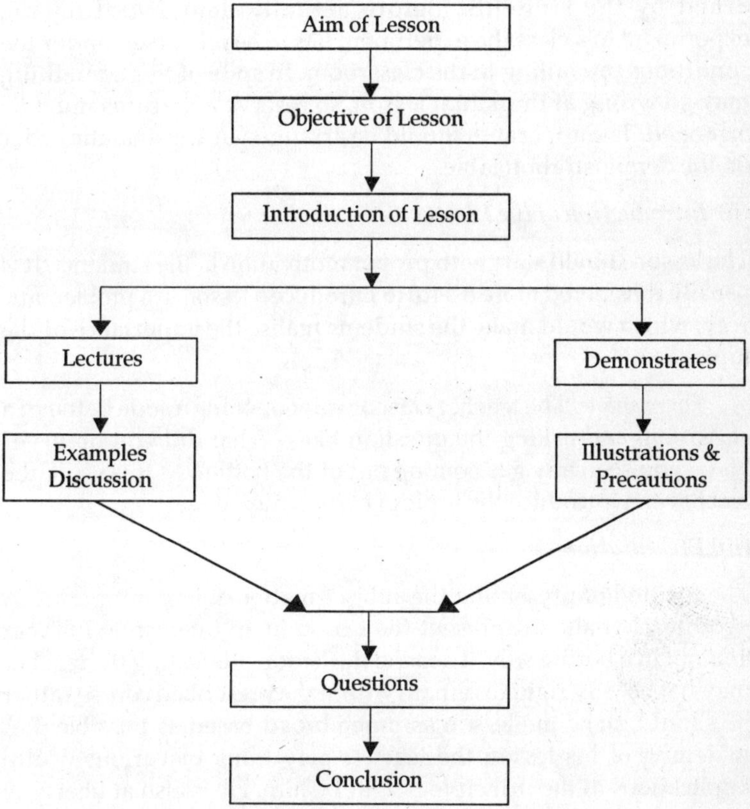


Shall we discuss the steps in detail?

***(i) Planning and Preparation***

A great care has to be taken by the teacher while planing and preparing his demonstration lesson. He should keep the following points in mind while preparing his lesson:

1. Subject-matter.
2. Questions to be asked.
3. Apparatus required for the experiment.

To achieve the above stated objective, the teacher should thoroughly go through the pages of the textbook, relevant to the lesson. After this the teacher should prepare the lesson plan by including include the principles to be explained, a list of experiments to be demonstrated and the type of questions to be asked by the students. Before actually demonstrating the experiment to a class the experiment has to be rehearsed under the conditions prevailing in the classroom. In spite of this something may go wrong at the actual lesson, so reserve apparatus must be arranged. The apparatus should be arranged in a systematic order on the demonstration table.

***(ii) Introduction of the Lesson***

The lesson should start with proper motivation to the students. It is usually considered more useful to introduce a lesson in a problematic way, which would make the students realise the importance of the topic.

*For example:* The teacher can consider opening a soda bottle in a classroom and asking the question like—What did you observe? Have you seen any gas coming out of the bottle? At this stage the teacher can introduce the topic of carbon dioxide.

***(iii) Presentation***

The method of presenting the subject-matter is very important. A good teacher should present the lesson in an interesting manner and not in a boring way. To make the lesson interesting the teacher may not be very rigid to remain within the prescribed course rather he should make the lesson as much broad based as possible. For widening of his lesson the teacher may think of various useful applications of the principle taught by him. He is also at liberty to take examples and illustrations from other allied branches of science to make the lesson more interesting. The life history and some interesting facts from the life of the great scientist whose name is associated with the topic under discussion can also be cited to make the lesson interesting. Thus, every effort should be made to present the matter in a lively and interesting manner and a lesson should never be presented as 'dry bones' of an academic course. In a lesson dealing with Archimedes principle, we should not feel satisfied just by stating the principle and then demonstrating it with one or two experiments rather he should discuss its applications in daily life such as ships, floating bodies, diving and rising of submarines, the use of pictures, posters, diagrams, slides, films etc., in addition to experiments to illustrate the topic in hand.

Constant questions and answers should form part of every demonstration lesson. Questions and cross-questions are essential for properly illustration of the principle being discussed. Questions need to be in such a way that their answers from a complete teaching unit. Though an effort be made to encourage the students to answer a large number of questions but if students fails to answer some questions teacher should provide the answers to such questions. It is unwise to expect all the answers from the pupil and a teacher should feel satisfied if he has been able to create a desire in a student to know what he does not know. The lesson should be presented in a clear voice and the teacher should speak with correct pronunciation. He should avoid the use of any bombastic and ambiguous terms. The continuous talk is likely to lead to monotony and to avoid experiments should be well-spaced throughout the lesson.

***(iv) Performance of Experiments***

A good observer has been described as a person who has learned to use his senses of touch, sight, smell and hearing in an intelligent and alert manner. Don't we want children to observe what happens in experiments and to have ample opportunities to state their observations carefully? We also want them to try to explain what happens in reference to their problem, but we want to make certain. There is separation between observations and generalization and conclusions. We will be violating the true spirit of science if we allow children to generalise from one experiment of observation.

The following steps are generally accepted as valuable in developing and concluding science experiments with the children:

- Write the problems to be solved in simple words so that everyone understands.
- Make a list of activities that will be used to solve problems.
- Gather material for conducting experiments.
- Work out a format of the steps in the order of procedure so that everyone knows what is to be done.
- The teacher should always try the experiment well in advance to become acquainted with the equipment and procedure.
- Record the findings in ways commensurate with the maturity level and purposes of the student.

- Assist students in making generalisations from conclusions only after sufficient evidence and experiences.
- The demonstration experiment should be presented by the teacher in a methodical way. He should work in a tidy, clean and orderly manner while demonstrating experiment. Some of the important points to be kept in mind while demonstrating an experiment are as under:
- Experiments should be simple and speedy.
- The experiments must work and their results should be clear and striking.
- Experiments be properly spaced throughout the lesson.
- Keep some reserve apparatus on the demonstration table.
- Keep the demonstration apparatus intact till it has to be used again.

**Black Board Summary**

A summary of important results and principles must be written on the black board. Use of black board should also be frequently made for drawing necessary sketches and diagrams. The black board summary should be written in neat, clean and legible way. Black board summary is an index to a teacher's ability. Let us recall the points we should keep in mind while writing on a black board:

- Proper space should be left between different letters and words.
- We should always start writing from left-hand corner of the black board.
- Care should be taken to start a new line only when the first one has extended across the black board.
- We need to take care not to divide the words at the end of a line.
- We should make all efforts to keep all the paragraphs and similar signs in calculations under one another.
- While drawing sketches and diagrams we should preferably use single lined' diagrams.
- All the diagrams drawn on the board should be properly labelled.

**Supervision**

Students need to be asked to take the complete notes of the black board summary including the sketches and diagrams drawn. Such a record will be quite helpful to the students for learning the lesson.

Such a summary will prove beneficial only if it has been copied correctly from the black board and to make sure that students are copying the black board summary properly. Teacher should make sure of it by frequently going to the seats of the students.

### *Common Errors in a Lecture Demonstration Lesson*

A summary of common errors committed while delivering a demonstration lesson is given below:

1. The apparatus may not be ready for use.
2. There may not be an apparent relation between the demonstration experiment and the topic under discussion.
3. Black board summary may not be up to the mark.
4. Teacher may be in a hurry to arrive at generalisation without allowing sufficient time to arrive at these generalisations from facts.
5. Teacher may sometimes fail to ask right type of questions.
6. Teacher sometimes may use difficult words or language.
7. Teacher may sometime talk more which may mar the enthusiasm of the students.
8. Teacher may not give sufficient time for recording data etc.
9. Teacher has not given proper attention to supervision.
10. Probably this list should serve as a ready reckoned while we are conducting an experiment and help us to minimise the errors.

### *Merits of Lecture Demonstration Method*

Following are the merits of this method:

1. It is an economical method as compared to purely student centered approaches.
2. It is a psychological method and students take active interest in teaching learning process.
3. It leads students from concrete to abstract situation and thus is more psychological.
4. It is a suitable method if the apparatus to be handled is costly and sensitive and such an apparatus is likely to damage if handled by students.
5. This method can be safer if the experiments to be demonstrated are dangerous or which needs special care.
6. In comparison to Heuristic method, project method etc., it is time saving but lecture method is too speedy.

7. It can be used successfully *for* all types *of* students.
8. In this method such experiments which are difficult for students can be included.
9. This method can be used to impart manual and manipulative skills to students.
10. It is a suitable method when there is less number of apparatus required to students' size.

*Limitations of Lecture Demonstration Method*

Some of the limitations of this method are as under:

1. It provides no scope for 'learning by doing' for students as students just observe what the teacher is performing. Thus students fail to relish the joys of direct personal experience.
2. Since the teacher performs the experiment in his own pace, many students cannot comprehend the concept being clarified.
3. Since the method is not child centered so it makes no provision for individual differences. All types of students including slow learners and genius have to proceed with the same speed.
4. It fails to impart training in scientific attitude.
5. In this method students many a times fail to observe many finer details of the apparatus used because they observe it from a distance.

## HISTORICAL METHOD

### Introduction

The historical method of teaching science developed out of a concern that although each student would not be expected to become a scientist, but each citizen should have some understanding the role of physical science and scientists play in determining public policy and allocating public resources. In this approach, students are exposed to a series of case stories, which attempt to show how context, concept, process and individual creativity of scientists have combined to establish what is known as the "structure of the scientific disciplines." This method if employed successfully gives depth to students understanding because every scientific idea has its own past history. It provides students with the inside story of science from an emotive angle. Even the crude attempts made at forming hypotheses, setting up controlling experiments and narrating inferences can be informative.

A resourceful teacher can bridge the gap between present and past knowledge and make the present interesting by recalling past anecdotes.

**Approaches of Historical Method**

There are several ways of using this method while teaching physical science. We shall discuss some feasible approaches in the classroom:

*(i) The Anecdotal Approach*

As teachers we can start the lesson with an interesting incident or anecdotes from the lives of scientists leading to a particular scientific discovery such as Archimedes and Eureka, or Newton and the ripe apple falling down.

*(ii) The Biographical Approach*

The complete study of the life history and work contributed by scientists such as Raman, Faraday, Lavoisier, Rutherford etc., would be really useful to the students. It would enable the students to look into their life and project themselves onto the life experiences of scientists. They would be able to experience success and frustrations as they learn their biographies and appreciate their hopes and disappointments.

*(iii) The Evolutionary Approach*

According to this approach, different theories arranged in a chronological order may be presented as they were developed. When teaching the lesson on Oxygen we may trace back to the 'Phlogiston theory' and deal with the contribution of Priestly and Lavoisier. From there on we can reach the modern methods of preparing oxygen and its use in industry etc., linking the present topic with the historical background. This approach can be applied to topics like theories of light, or the evolution of classifications of the elements etc.

*(iv) The Social Approach*

Scientists have often engaged themselves in tackling the problems of immediate importance and interest to the society. The potentialities of Atomic Energy for destruction and peaceful purposes are the best example of science and social relations. Similarly with space research, science has brought a great revolution in the system of communication.

## Application of Historical Method

Let us think of a few instances where historical method can be used:

For example, a teacher can use the life of Sir C. V. Raman to inspire students. We can narrate the story of his early childhood and emphasise how despite lack of opportunity, his small stature and ill-health, he could excel in life. We can also focus on the fact that inspite of better offers for professional advancement abroad, Prof Raman chose to stay in India and pursued his research with the material available here. This will help students to imbibe qualities of confidence, perseverance, hard work, optimism etc. They may be motivated to become scientists and may improve their performance in schools.

'Principle of Archimedes': To arouse interest in students towards a relatively difficult concept we can narrate the story of Archimedes and Eureka.

In fact, while discussing about most inventions like Newton's gravitational law, Einsteins Relativity, Telescope, Television etc., we can present the historical sketch.

We can find a good number of chemists whose life story could prove very interesting for example, Louis Pasteur, Priestly, Lavoisier etc.

### *Advantages of Historical Method*

Let us see what the chief advantages of using this method are:

*(i)* Science is viewed in this approach as an evolving area of study, which is tentative and subjective which is the real nature of science.

*Example:* Newton's corpuscular theory of light was replaced by Huygens wave theory to explain interference and diffraction. Today, we use quantum mechanics to explain dual nature of light. Hence, while discussing about nature of light; the historical description of development of theories will make the study interesting.

*(ii)* Science is a humanistic endeavour and students

understand humanness of science. The relation between science and society can be made explicit using this method.

### *Limitations of Historical Method*

1. It is a very difficult job for the science teachers to link the past thinking in science with the current thinking.
2. It is very difficult to find relevant case histories for different age groups.
3. Inclusion of historical aspects will increase the burden of children as their syllabus is already heavy.
4. It is not suitable for a vast number of topics.

## Student Centered Methods

### *(i) Heuristic Method*

'Heuristic' means 'Discovery' in Greek. It is derived from the Greek word 'Heuriskin'. Prof. H. E. Armstrong advocated this method. Prof. Armstrong said the following about the method "Heuristic method is a method of teaching which involves our placing the students as far as possible in the attitude of a discoverer." So this method excites children to work and think for themselves.

Rybur W.M. says, "This method as the name implies is a method by which the pupils discover things for him. The pupil is put in the position of a pioneer and finds the way along the path of knowledge as those who first discovered the facts, principles and laws which are now known to all."

The procedure inherent in Heuristic approach is very simple. A sheet of instruction concerning the problem is given to every pupil. There is expected to make observations to conduct experiments as the case may be in accordance with the instruction. Then the student records the observations in notebook. From the observations, it is expected to draw conclusions or inferences. He is finally introduced to reasoning her/his own observations or experiments. In this manner student is encouraged to learn independently through his own investigation.

Thus, the main objective of Heuristic method is "To make pupils more exact, more truthful, observant, thoughtful, dexterous, to lay the foundation for future self-education and to encourage the growth of a spirit of inquiry and research. "In their daily life, the students face so many problems and they try to solve them by gathering information from different sources. Thus, there is no spoon feeding on part of the teacher and in this manner students get training in scientific method or attacking and solving a problem.

Westway has aptly remarked, "Essentially, the Heuristic Method is intended to provide training in method and knowledge is a secondary consideration all together."

*Procedure to be Adopted in Using Heuristic Method*

We have represented the steps in lecture and lecture demonstration method. Similarly we will diagrammatically represent the steps to be followed in adopting Heuristic method?

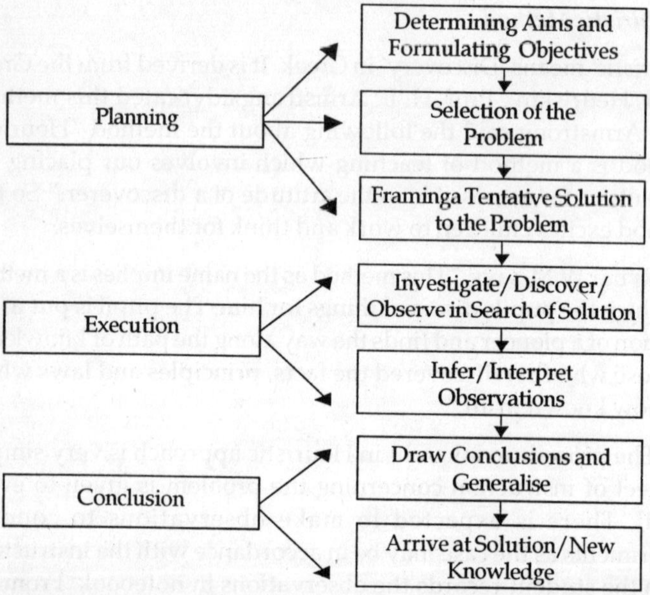


A problem is assigned to the class and each child is made to feel responsible for finding out solution by ones own self. Each child tries to acquire information about the problem from different sources. The child is free to move about and discuss the problem with the classmates. Each student is given a sheet of instructions regarding the problem in hand. The student can get guidance from the teacher. The teacher should try to induce answers from students by raising as many questions as possible. In this way they interpret their observations and finally draw relevant conclusions.

*Role of the Teacher in Implementing Heuristic Method*

Shall we try to find out what our role is in adopting this method?

1. The teacher is the hub around which the success or failure of this method rests. The role the teacher has to play is :
2. The teacher should help the student to search for a suitable problem. Here the teacher should keep in mind the age, ability and level of the student, along with the facilities available.
3. The teacher should act as a guide and instructor to the students by providing sufficient background information and help the students to get going.
4. Detailed instruction sheets should be given to the students and hence the teacher has to take pains in developing the instruction sheets.
5. The teacher by allowing freedom of thought and action would enable the development of values and attitudes consistent with science among students.
6. Arrangement for supplementing the students knowledge should be made by teacher like library facilities, field trips etc.
7. A gifted teacher would be ever ready to help the students to draw inferences from their experiments and observations. The teacher should assist in relating these inferences to the body of knowledge they already have gained.
8. The teacher should possess curiosity, interest and spirit of scientific investigation because they are to be developed in the child. Unless a teacher is a discoverer we cannot expect that the children under the guidance to form an attitude of a discoverer.

*Advantages of Heuristic Method*

We have discussed about the salient features of Heuristic method. These are the utility of Heuristic method in teaching of physical science:

1. The method stresses individual's practical work, careful observation and independent thinking which makes a child self-reliant.
2. It imparts knowledge of scientific method of thinking and inculcates scientific attitude among students.

3. The heuristic method is based on the important psychological principle of learning by doing.
4. Individual differences can be catered to, as each student can work at his own pace.
5. Students develop research skills, including setting up and fitting apparatus, conducting experiments, habits of neatness and patience are acquired.
6. Students become self-confident since they learn through self-activity.
7. The probability of concepts and facts being retained for a long time is more because the child learns from direct experiences.
8. It prepares a student for life by giving the ability to tackle and solve any problem of life scientifically.

*Limitations of Heuristic Method*

In spite of all the advantages listed in the last section the method has some limitations. They are:

1. This method is feasible only with a gifted teacher and a small class. Both these basic requisites are difficult to attain practically.
2. Suitable textbooks are not available and difficult to write.
3. It is very uneconomical in terms of time. It will be difficult for a teacher to complete the syllabus in time.
4. In this method skills are supposed to be learnt at the expense of knowledge. But acquisition of knowledge is equally important.
5. This method involves experimentation hence there is need for infrastructure which is a costly affair.
6. The heuristic method expects too much from the students. Probably all students cannot cope with this method.
7. The method is not suitable for all classes.
8. Practical problems like time-table adjustment make it difficult to adopt it in the school curriculum.

***(ii) Project Method***

*Definition and Nature*

Project means something that has been planned or a plan of a scheme or an undertaking.

According to Dr. Kilpatrick "A project is a unit of whole hearted purposeful activity carried on preferably, in its natural setting." According to Stevenson," A project is a problematic act carried to its completion in its natural setting" and according to Ballard, "A project is a bit of real life that has been incorporated into the school."

Tomas and Long give a modified definition of project. They defined it as "A voluntary undertaking which involves constructive effort or thought and eventuates into objective results."

A project should arise out of a need felt by pupils and it should never be forced on them. It should be purposeful and significant. It should look important and must be interesting. For this the teacher should always be on the lookout to identify new situations that arise and discuss them with students to identify their interests. Situations may be provided by different methods. Some such methods may include talking to students on the topics of common interest e.g., how did they spend their holidays, what did they study in a science exhibition, a planetarium etc.

From various definitions of an educational project we get the following underlying ideas:

*(a)* School tasks are to be as real and as purposeful as the tasks of wider life beyond the school walls.

*(b)* They are of such a nature that the pupil is genuinely eager to carry them out in order to achieve a desirable and clearly realised aim.

*(c)* A project should have:

- a purpose
- a plan
- an activity
- rich experience
- natural setting or reality.

According to Kilpatrick, "The part of the pupil and the part of the teacher, in most of the school work, depends largely on who does the proposing." The teacher should refrain from proposing any project otherwise the whole purpose of the method would be defeated. Teacher should only tempt the students for a particular project by providing a situation but the proposal for the project should finally come from students. The teacher must exercise guidance in selection of the project and if the students make an unwise choice, the teacher should tactfully guide them for a better project.

*Qualities of a Good Project*

The essential qualities of a good project are:

(i) It should have evident worth for the individual or the group that undertakes it.
(ii) The project must have a bearing on a great number of subjects and the knowledge acquired through it may be applicable in a variety of ways.
(iii) The project should be timely.
(iv) The project should be challenging.
(v) The project should be feasible.

It is for the teacher to see that the purpose of the project is clearly defined and understood. Considering various definitions of project we may consider it as a kind of life experience which is an outcome of a craving or desire of the pupils. This is a method of spontaneous and incidental teaching. "Learning by living" may be a better meaning of project method, because life is full of projects and individuals carry out these projects in their everyday life in a routine manner.

*Principles of Project Method*

Project method has originated out of the pioneering work of Dewey and Stevenson. As we have seen in the earlier section of this method, the students select a problem in consultation with a teacher and then develop through discussion the plan of action and the type of material and equipment required for its execution. Students learn through cooperation and active participation in the implementation of the action strategy planned.

Project method is based on the following principles:

(i) *Principle of activity*—Learning by doing.
(ii) *Principle of experience/reality*—Learning by living.
(iii) *Principle of active participation*—Individually and in Groups
(iv) *Principles of group work*—Children learn better through association, cooperation and activity.
(v) *Principle of utility*—Usually projects are chosen that have immediate relevance to the students.

(vi) *Principle of freedom*—Students are allowed to work independently without much interference from the teacher.
(vii) Principle of correlation.
(viii) Principle of economy.

**Types of Projects**

Different types of projects with examples for each are presented below:

**1. *General Classification***

Generally projects are classified into six types as:

(i) Individual project.
(ii) Group projects.
(iii) Construction projects.
(iv) Investigatory projects.
(v) Verification projects.
(vi) Display projects.

*(i) Individual Project*

This is similar to individual research wherein a student is motivated to do something on his own. Care is taken to see that the project is challenging enough but is not beyond the level of the student.

*(ii) Group Projects*

In this type a group of students select a project and work for it collectively and by distributing work among them. Choices of topic, number and members of group have to be so chosen that they work in group.

*(iii) Construction Projects*

In such projects the pupils build/construct/produce something at the end of their project. The final product may be working model (motor, peirscope and telescope) or a structural model (atomic structure, nuclear power plant). In the process of construction of the model the children learn a lot about the related topics.

*(iv) Investigatory Projects*

Science is a beehive of concepts. Students can probe into any one of them and produce a nice project report. In the process of investigation the students may consult reference books or perform experiments.

*(v) Verification Projects*

Any law or science principle can be verified by undertaking a project.

*(vi) Display Projects*

In this type of project some science topic is taken as the theme and charts, specimens' models, posters, graphs, photographs are developed regarding principles, concepts related to the theme and displayed.

**2. *Smith's Classification***

N.F. Smith has categorised science projects into following types:

*(i)* Model building – Atomic structure, volcanoes.

*(ii)* Hobby projects – Assembling electronic circuits like fire alarm.

*(iii)* Laboratory demonstrations directly from the textbook, or laboratory manual – distillation, electroplating.

*(iv)* Report and poster projects from literature research – car, use of pesticides.

*(v)* Investigative projects in which the students are involved in critical thinking, and science processes like measuring and inferring.

**3. *Kilpatrick's Classification***

Kilpatrick has classified projects on the basis of task involved:

*(i)* *Practical tasks – (to embody some idea, or plan in external form):* In this type of project the producer's type emphasis is directed towards the actual construction of material, object or article

*(ii)* *Appreciation – (to enjoy some experience):* In this type – the consumer's type, the objective is to obtain direct or vicarious experiences , such as listening to stories or reading.

*(iii)* *Problem solving (to solve problems):* In this type – the problem type – the chief purpose to obtain involving the intellectual processes, such as determining the density of a certain liquid.

*(iv)* *Mastery of a skill, knowledge. (to obtain some action or degree of skill or knowledge):* In this type – the drill type – the objective is to attain a certain degree of skill.

**Steps in Project Method**

For completing a project we have six stages in actual practice and as usual we shall represent these in a flow chart.

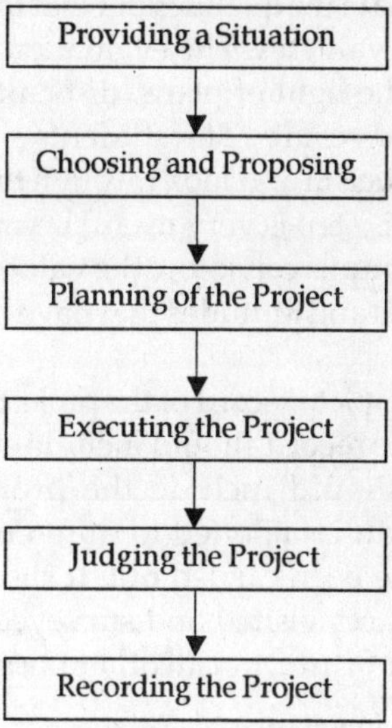


We shall discuss each of these steps in detail:

- *Planning:* The students are encouraged by the teacher to plan out the details of the project. In the process of planning teacher has to act only as a guide and give suggestions at times but actual planning is left to the students.
- *Execution:* Once the project has been chosen and the details of the project have been planned, the teacher role is to only help the students in executing the project according to the plan. Since execution of a project is the longest step in the project method so it need a lot of patience on the part of the students and the teacher. During this step the teacher needs to carefully supervise the pupils in manipulative skills to prevent waste of material and to keep a check against accidents. The teacher should supervise the assignment of work to different students and ensure that it is in accordance with their tastes, interests, aptitudes and capabilities. Teacher should take care to see that every member of the group gets a chance to do something. The teacher should

keep track of the progress of the project and check if project is being worked out as per the chalked out plans.

- *Evaluation:* Periodic evaluation of the project should be undertaken both by the pupils and the teachers. The pupils should estimate the qualities of what they have done before the teacher evaluates. The evaluation of the project has to be done in the light of plans, difficulties in the execution and achieved results. The students should be allowed to have self-criticism and look through their own failings and findings. This step is very useful because as a result of the project, the pupils can know the values of the information, interest, skills and attitudes that have been modified by the project.
- *Record:* A complete record of the project has to be kept by the students. The record should include every thing about the project. It should include the proposal, plan and its discussion, duties allotted to different students and how far they have been carried out. It should also include the details of places visited and surveyed, maps etc., drawn, guidance for future and all other possible details.

### *Examples of Projects in Science*

Here are given some projects for a science class:

- Our food
- Our atmosphere
- Water
- Air
- Sources of electrical energy
- Energy conversions
- Environmental pollution
- Alternative renewable sources of energy.

### Sample Project on Water

Let us now consider an interesting project on the study of water. The entire class can be divided into four to six groups to study the various facets of this project: "how we get our water, biology and the water supply, government and the water supply, and water in the home." Each facet can be further specified with regard to the amount of work involved, method of procedure, and the number of pupils needed in the group to accomplish the task in the available time period. Groups can be of variable size and, as far as possible, the members of a particular group should share the same interest. The work involved in this project could probably be as follows:

| | |
|---|---|
| *Group A:* | Various sources of water with general reference to the existence of the water cycle in nature. |
| *Group B:* | Water (pure, hard and soft) : Physical and chemical properties.<br>Methods of purifying water including removal of hardness. |
| *Group C :* | Impact of water on plant and animal life including human beings. Our responsibilities as citizens in the use and conservation of water. |
| *Group D :* | Some sort of participation in activities like map reading and drawing, making of a sand table map and relief map with clay and pictorial representation of local rocks. |
| *Group E :* | Local geology and its effect on the water supply. |
| *Group F :* | Water conservation techniques. |

Each group can be asked to illustrate their reports with actual specimens, models, pictures, brief historical references and diagrams.

**Role of Teacher**

In the conduct of this method a teacher has a very important role to play:

- In project method of teaching the role of a teacher is that of a guide, friend and philosopher.
- He helps the students in solving their problems just like an elder brother. He encourages his students to work collectively and amicably in the group.
- He also helps his students to avoid mistakes.
- He makes it a point that each member of the group contributes something to the completion of the project and in this process helps the shy and weaker students to work along with their classmates.
- If the students face failure during execution of some steps of the project the teacher should not execute any portion of the project but should only explain to his students the reasons of their failure and should suggest them some better methods or techniques that may be used by them next time for the success of the project.
- During the execution stage teacher also learns something as a co-operating partner.

- Teacher should always remain alert and active during execution step and see that the project is completed as planned.
- During execution of the project teacher should maintain a democratic atmosphere.
- Teacher must be well-read and well-informed so that he can help the students to the successful completion of the project.

*Merits of the Project Method*

- It is a method of teaching based on psychological laws of learning. The learning is related to child's life and he acquires it through meaningful activity.
- It imbibes the spirit of cooperation, as it is a cooperative venture. Teacher and students join in the project.
- It stimulates interest in natural as also man made situations. Moreover, the interest is spontaneous and not under compulsion.
- The method provides opportunities for pupils of different abilities and aptitudes to work with in the framework of the same scheme.
- It upholds the dignity of labour.
- It brings about a close correlation between a particular activity and various subjects.
- It is a problem solving method and places very less emphasis on cramming or memorising.
- It helps to inculcate social discipline through joint activities of the teacher and the taught.
- A project can be used to arouse interest in a particular topic as it blends school life with outside world. It provides situations in which the students come in direct contact with their environment.
- It develops self-confidence and self-discipline.
- A project tends to illustrate the real nature of the subject.
- A project affords opportunity to develop keenness and accuracy of observation and produces a spirit of inquiry.
- It puts a challenge to the students and thus stimulates constructive and creative thinking.
- It provides the students an opportunity for mutual exchange of ideas.
- This method helps the children to organise their knowledge.

***Limitations of the Project Method***

- Projects require a lot of time and this method can be used as a part of science work only.
- Though the method provides the student superficial knowledge of so many things it provides insufficient knowledge of some fundamental principles.
- In the project planning and execution of the project the teacher is required to put in much more work in comparison to other methods of teaching.
- The teacher has been assumed as master of all subjects, which is practically not possible.
- It is an expensive method as it involves tours, excursions, purchase of apparatus and equipment etc.
- The method of organising instruction is unsystematic and thus the regular time-table of work will be upset.
- It underestimates man's power of imagination, which enables to savour the full experience of another without the necessity of undergoing the experience himself.
- Sometimes the projects may be too ambitious and beyond pupils capacity to accomplish.
- Larger projects in hands of an inexperienced teacher lead to boredom.
- The education given by projects is likely to emphasise relationships in breadth than in depth.

## LABORATORY METHOD

### Meaning of Laboratory Method

Science laboratory work is a unique way of instruction which is an integral part of science teaching. It helps students to understand complex, abstract ideas and gives students an opportunity to participate in and have an appreciation for the methods of science. It helps students to investigate and verify scientific concepts, principles, and laws by themselves.

Students can be stuffed with facts and theories but without experiments they cannot experience the reality of physics or chemistry as a science. The development of powers of observation, measurement, inferences etc all depend on laboratory work.

Thus, we can say that if the teacher performs an experiment, it is a 'Demonstration' and if pupils perform it, it is called 'Laboratory

Method' and when each individual works independently on his own it is 'Individual Laboratory Method'. This method enables pupils 'to do' rather than 'see'. Students are active participants in this method in contrast to lecture method where they are passive spectators or observers.

John Dewey said the following about science laboratory: "In the hands of a good teacher, it is in itself an excellent vehicle for instruction. It gives an insight into authentic science. It is intellectually exacting. It requires careful attention during planning, execution and observation. It demands interpretation and abstraction. Most students enjoy it. It couples cognitive activities with hands on, action oriented, concrete operational activities. It is a stimulating change from lectures and other forms of instruction."

It is inter disciplinary. It teaches students skills in reading and writing applying mathematics to real problems, classify measuring, interpreting, extrapolating, drawing inferences, framing hypotheses, building mathematical, verbal and physics models. It helps students to develop manual dexterity, patience, dependability and a spirit of co-operation. It helps to enhance and strengthen student-student and student-teacher interpersonal relations.

A learning laboratory is a busy laboratory. Although it is time consuming for students and mentally and physically taxing for teachers, laboratory work is indispensable—if the spirit of science is to be conveyed to the younger generation and if they are to develop the capacity for independent thinking and learning. The laboratory is a discovery of the conditions under which labour may become intellectually fruitful and not merely productive.

### Aims of Laboratory Method

The aims of laboratory method in teaching physical science are:

- *(i)* Illustration of abstract scientific understandings.
- *(ii)* Development of scientific concepts and principles.
- *(iii)* Development of scientific skills.
- *(iv)* Awakening and maintenance of curiosity about the environment.

### The Purpose of the Laboratory Method

Science concepts and principles can be taught by this method to fulfill the following purposes:

*(i)* To encourage accurate observation.
*(ii)* To develop manipulative skills.
*(iii)* To train students in the scientific method.
*(iv)* To develop scientific curiosity.

## Organisation of Laboratory Work

Laboratory work can be organised in the following ways:

*(i)* *Even front System:* In this system all the students are asked to do the same experiment at a time individually.
*(ii)* *Group System:* In this system one group of students will be doing the same experiment.
*(iii)* *Rotation System:* In this system the above two systems are combined. The class is divided into five or six groups. Each group will be doing different experiments and by rotation all the groups will be completing all experiments within a specific period of time.

## Approaches for Laboratory Work

The various approaches for laboratory work are:

1. Free exploration.
2. Unstructured exploration.
3. Structured inductive experiment.
4. Deductive – verification experiment.
5. Science process oriented.
6. Technical skill oriented.

Shall we compare the different laboratory approaches:

| *Sl.No.* | *Student Experience* | *Classification* | *Outcome* |
|---|---|---|---|
| 1. | Students are given two magnets iron filings and are asked to determine something about it | Free Exploration | Possibly identifies poles of a magnet at the ends where filings are attracted most |
| 2. | Students are given two magnets with North and South poles marked and asked to determine something about it. | Unstructured Exploration | Identifies that like poles repel and unlike poles attract |
| 3. | Students are given a magnet and a compass and they are to experiment by bringing it near the magnet. | Structured Inductive Experiments | Students learn that compass points to the North pole of the magnet. |

*(Contd.)*

| *Sl.No.* | *Student Experience* | *Classification* | *Outcome* |
|---|---|---|---|
| 4. | Students are given two magnets and asked to verify the law of poles by bringing like poles and unlike poles closer | Deductive Verification Experiment | Students verify that N-N and S-S repel N-S and S-N attract, i.e. like poles repel and unlike poles attract. |
| 5. | Students are given Vernier calipers and asked to take readings and find the length of an object. | Science Process Oriented | Students learn process skills of observing, tabulating and experimenting. |
| 6. | Students are asked to focus a telescope or draw a liquid from a pipette | Technical Skill Oriented | Students acquire manipulative skills that develop hand – eye coordination. |

## Types of Laboratory Experiments

There are five types of laboratory experiment that we could take up. Can you list them? They are:

(i) *Illustrative Experiments:* These experiments are done to illustrate a scientific principle .Ex: To illustrate Newton's third law of motion, various action reaction experiments can be taken up.

(ii) *To Find Numerical Values for Physical Quantities:* Ex. To find g using simple pendulum

(iii) *Productive Experiments:* Experiments in which something is produced. Ex. To prepare oxygen in the laboratory

(iv) *Verification Experiments:* Experiments carried on to verify experimental results already obtained earlier. Ex. To verify Archimedes Principle.

(v) *Investigatory Experiments or Open-ended Experiments:* Experiments done with a purpose to investigate effect of some aspect. Ex. Effect of a detergent on different types of fabrics.

## Procedure to be Adopted to Use Laboratory Method

As usual shall, we represent the laboratory method in a block diagram form?

Laboratory activities must be well-organised and carefully planned. The science laboratory exercises and orients them to the

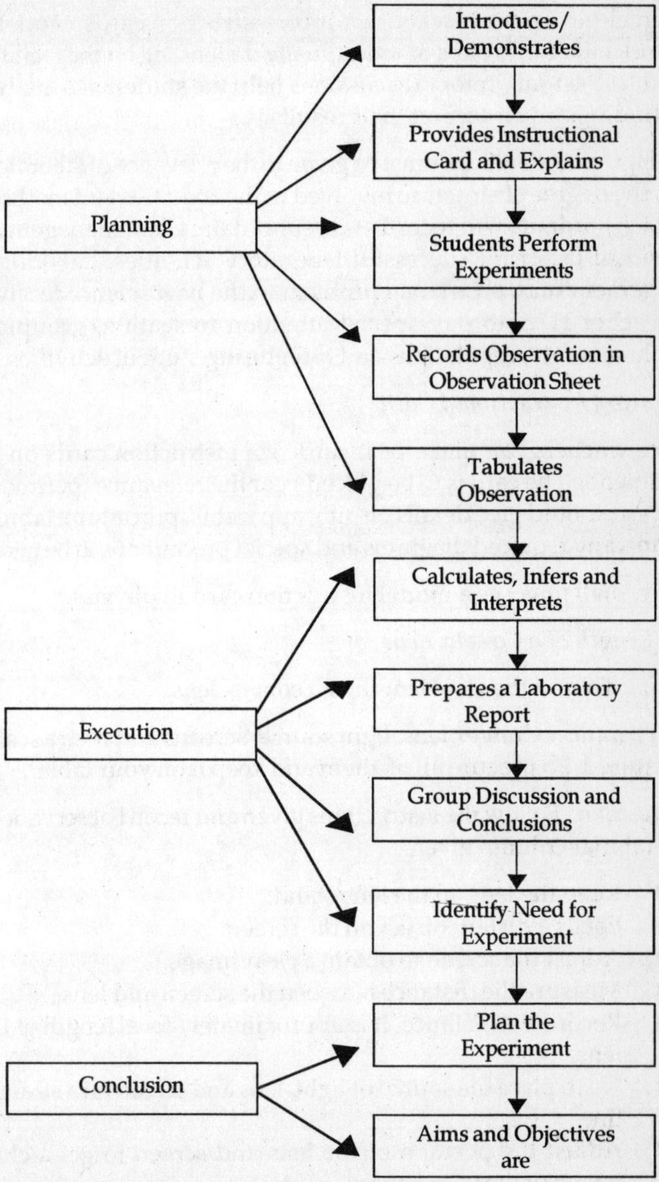


objectives to be attained and the procedures to be adopted. Necessary directions should be given for actual laboratory work, highlighting the precautions to be taken. These instructions could be oral, or written either on the blackboard or on instruction cards. Students can work either in groups or individually depending on the facilities available. Post-laboratory discussions help the students to analyse their findings and interpret their results.

Major considerations must be given to the relevance of laboratory work, the degree of structure involved in the activities and methods by which students will record and report data. Class management is a critical factor for successful laboratory activities. Laboratory management may pose some problem to the new science teacher. The teacher HAS to pay special attention to seating, grouping, discipline, safety, regulations and monitoring student activities.

### *Laboratory Instructional Card*

Science teachers can make post card size instruction cards on all experiments. The card is to be placed near the relevant experiment. Each card should give details on aim, apparatus, procedure, tabular columns, any required diagrams and special precautions to be taken.

We shall now see a model instruction card in physics.

### *Focal Length of a Convex Lens*

*Aim:* To find the focal length of a convex lens.

*Apparatus:* Convex lens, light source, screens and metre scales are required. So procure all of them and keep it on your table.

*Procedure:* Follow the instructions given and record observations in the tabular column given:

- Keep the lens on the lens stand.
- Focus a distant object on the screen.
- Adjust the screen to obtain a clear image.
- Measure the distance between the screen and lens.
- Record the distance. It is approximately focal length of the lens.
- Next, place the source of light, lens and screen on a straight tine.
- Adjust the position of the lens and screen to get a clear image of the wire gauze.
- Measure the distance '$u$' between source and lens. Measure the distance '$v$' between the lens and screen.
- Record $u$ and $v$ in tabular column.

- Repeat experiment for different values of $u$ and $v$.
- Calculate the value of '$f$'
- Formula: $1/f = 1/u + 1/v$

*Observation Sheet*

The approximate value for f= – – – – cms

| *S. No.* | *U cm.* | *V cm.* | *UV cm* | *U+V cm.* | *F= UV/U+V cm.* |
|---|---|---|---|---|---|
| 1. | | | | | |
| 2. | | | | | |
| 3. | | | | | |
| 4. | | | | | |
| 5. | | | | | |

The focal length of convex lens = cm.

*Advantages of the Laboratory Method*

In this method, the 'hands-on' experiences provided to the students can be more or less controlled by the teacher. The advantages of using this method are:

*(i)* There is no doubt that the use of the laboratory to develop skills in the use of laboratory equipment is a worthy goal, which cannot be obtained without actual experience.
*(ii)* The laboratory method provides students with the opportunity to view science, as it is practiced rather than merely reading or hearing about it.
*(iii)* Students definitely require hands-on experience in order to grasp the significance of certain phenomenon.
*(iv)* Students gain real experience with the processes of science.
*(v)* The students get a chance of 'learning by doing'.
*(vi)* The students develop self-confidence and a sense of achievement.

*Limitations of the Laboratory Method*

It is difficult to identify limitations of the laboratory method. The problems encountered while using this method are:

*(i)* Laboratory skill development is a worth-while objective for the use of the laboratory method. As modern laboratories become more and more sophisticated in the use of

equipment, it is highly unlikely that the skills learnt in a secondary science laboratory will have a corresponding place in the work place as was the case not long ago.

*(ii)* The laboratory method is not an efficient means of learning new, factual information of the form that appears in external examinations.

*(iii)* Often resources are not available to present laboratory exercises, which truly present the phenomena of interest and the less than precise outcomes detract from the intended goals rather than embellish the students' view of science and the scientific process.

*(iv)* There is the strong possibility that a well-designed demonstration will be more beneficial than a poorly defined laboratory.

## PROBLEM SOLVING METHOD

### Definition of Problem Solving Method

It has been rightly said that life is nothing but a series of problems and science students encounter scientific problems. These problems provoke thinking, demand understanding and lead one to one solution. Problem solving begins as soon as a task oriented situation is presented for which the learner doesn't have a ready-made solution but has the essential basic information required in order to solve it. The method, which elicits such a response, is a problem solving method.

According to Risk, T.M., "Problem solving may be defined as planned attack upon a difficulty or perplexity for the purpose of finding a satisfactory solution." Risk further elaborates that problem solving teaching procedure is a process of raising a problem in the minds of students in such a way as to stimulate purposeful, reflective thinking in arriving at a rational solution.

James Ross defined problem solving as an educational device whereby the teacher and the pupils attempt in a conscious, planned, purposeful manner to arrive at an explanation or solution to some educationally significant difficulty.

Yokam, Gerald A. and Simpson, R. H. have defined problem solving method as a method in which a person uses the ability to solve the problems which confronts the individual, enables a person to exercise control over the activities and environment. Without it is at the mercy of nature and cannot make intelligent social progress.

According to Kekule problem solving is not a spontaneous, automatic activity. He says one has to work out for the solution of a problem independently or with someone's help. It is said that Kekule used to recommend to his students: "Boys sleep with the problem and learn to dream. Your problem is then more likely to be solved."

The desired outcomes of using this method are to develop:

*(i)* a curious mind alert to unfamiliar situation.

*(ii)* an investigatory spirit to form some plan of attack.

*(iii)* a courageous spirit and open mindedness to react to conclusions.

**Steps in Problem Solving Method**

Shall we represent the steps of problem solving method now?

The above steps are only guiding steps. It is not necessary that every problem should be solved using the above steps. The Step III may be eliminated, and for testing the hypotheses information from some other sources (reference book, journals, newspapers, discussions with some experts etc.) may be taken. Sometimes even Steps II and III both may be eliminated in problem solving method, and information from some other sources (mentioned above) may be used to find the solution of the problem.

**Role of Teacher in Problem Solving Method**

A teacher's role in training students to solve problems is equally simple and complex. It is simple if the teacher leaves everything to the immature minds. Most of the students will then not learn any thing and chaotic conditions are likely to prevail in the classroom and laboratory. The result may be that the method will find disfavour with the administrators, and even teachers themselves may become totally dissatisfied with it. The teacher's job is complex if he/she helps the pupils to discover problems and continually motivates them to carry on their struggle for seeking partial or full solutions of the problems on which they are engaged. He must be enterprising enough to be aware of the various answers students are likely to think about. He has to stop certain lines of investigation when the excitement is high, with a strong force. Both the teacher and the students have to work on a voyage of discovery, which is neither too complex nor too long. A much greater danger faces the teacher when he finds himself totally inadequate for the solution of a particular problem. His personal and conventional image, that he knows everything, is likely to be quickly demolished, and this would be personally embarrassing. Circumstances will compel the teacher to sharpen ingenuity continually as the years pass by. Hence, the demands on the teacher are complex. His professional gains are immense if he tries hard to capture their imagination through individual and collective endeavours. Then, he may, succeed to develop and reinforce problem solving behaviours, skills and procedures among his pupils in a permissive atmosphere.

**Practical Suggestions for Solving a Problem in the Classroom**

Some of the precautions to be taken while using the problem solving method in the classroom are:

*(i)* We have to first read the problem carefully and see what it demands.

*(ii)* After noting what has to be found out, we should see what is given in the problem.

*(iii)* Next, we must make a list of various ideas that may strike us while solving the problem.

*(iv)* Then these ideas are tested against the given data. We have to identify if any of the ideas are helpful.

*(v)* If not, see whether to restructure the problem or even solve part of the problem.

*(vi)* Find out if a problem similar to it has been solved before? If so, how was it solved?

*(vii)* Then make a list of ideas, which appear to be promising. We can also take help of auxiliary relationships or constructions as in geometry.

*(viii)* Next, we plan the approach for tackling the problem. We select that line of approach or idea to explain part of the data or remove the real difficulty inherent in the problem.

*(ix)* Then that single idea (or ideas) is a possible solution to the problem and has been obtained organically.

**Inductive Approach to Problem Solving**

*Meaning of Inductive Approach*

Science is usually taught as laws and theories illustrated by phenomena. The educationists recommend that science should be taught as phenomena, theories and laws. They advocate the inductive approach for the teaching. The inductive approach to problem solving provides students with a learning situation in which they can discover a concept or principle. In this approach, generalisations are drawn from particulars, principles from observed phenomena, and rules from instances.

### *Steps in Inductive Problem Solving Approach*

The following are the steps to be followed while using inductive approach to problem solving:

The students explicitly define the problem. They then examine all aspects of the situation. The students collect a lot of relevant information from various sources namely books, laboratories, factories etc. The information collected is organised with the help of the teacher. Students frame possible solutions using the organised information. The students retain plausible solutions and the rest are rejected. The solutions are applied to the problem situation and the results are checked. The procedure is repeated until a correct solution is obtained.

The inductive approach to problem solving should be carefully planned. Efforts should be made in order to enable the students, especially students with low ability to recognise the relevant cues, provided in the situation. Through the inductive method student interest and motivation in science, can be appreciably increased, provided the right conditions prevail, which are:

- *(i)* students should have the prerequisite knowledge and skills, and
- *(ii)* there is not much irrelevant information cluttering the problem situation.

### *Examples of Inductive Approach to Problem Solving*

Let us think of few examples to solve problems inductively.

*Problem 1:* To find the relationship between the angle of deviation and the angle between two mirrors.

The teacher provides some hypothetical data, "A ray of light falls successively on two plane mirrors held at an angle and suffers reflection twice. The problem is to find out the factors on which the angle of deviation depends."

The students set up the apparatus and collect data and test it against assumed hypothesis. Through repeated trials the student will arrive at the general rule that "The angle of deviation is equal to twice the angle between the mirrors and is independent of the angle of incidence."

*Problem 2:* To find out action of acids on blue litmus paper.

The student takes a piece of blue litmus paper and dips it in Hydrochloric acid and observes the change in colour (it turns red). The student repeats the experiment with other acids in different test tubes (Ex. Sulphuric acid, Nitric acid, Acetic acid, Oxalic acid etc., in each case blue litmus turns red).

From the above experiments students make a generalisation that "acids turn blue litmus to red."

*Merits of the Inductive Method*

Shall we list the advantages of using inductive method?

They are:

- It helps understanding.
- It is a scientific method.
- It develops scientific attitude.
- It is a logical method and develops critical thinking and habit of keen observation.
- It is a method with psychological base and provides ample opportunities for student activities.
- The method is based on actual observations, thinking, and experimentation.
- It sustains student's interest because they move from known to unknown.
- It curbs the tendency to learn by rote and also reduces homework.
- It develops self-confidence.
- It develops the habit of intelligent hard work.

*Limitations of Inductive Method*

The method has a few drawbacks also can you think of them? They are:

(i) It is limited in range and cannot be used in solving and understanding all the topics in science.

(ii) The generalization obtained from a few observations is not the complete study of the topic. To fix the topic in the mind of the learner a lot of supplementary work and practice is needed.

(iii) Inductive reasoning is not absolutely conclusive. There are exceptions to every rule and also certain limitations.

(iv) It is a time consuming and laborious method.

(v) This method can be used only when there are rules to be learnt.

## Deductive Method of Problem Solving

### *Meaning and Nature of Deductive Method*

The most widely used approach in science teaching is the deductive approach. Deductive method is just opposite to inductive method. In this method the students are given the rule first and then shown the examples. In this method the learner proceeds from a general rule to a particular instance or from an abstract concept to concrete examples. Thus in this method facts are deduced or analysed by the application of established formula or experimentation. In this method, the formula or rule is accepted without argument as a duly established fact.

In this method, the teacher announces the topics of the day and he also gives the relevant formula/rule/law/principle etc. The law/formula is also explained to the students with the help of examples, which are solved, on the board. From these the students get the idea of use or application of the concerned law/principle/formula. Then the problems are given to the students who solve the problems following the same method as explained to them earlier by the teacher. Students also memorises the results for further application.

### *Steps of Deductive Method of Problem Solving*

We shall now represent the steps to be followed while using deductive approach to problem solving.

The students first understand the problem. The students understand the concepts involved and define them clearly. Students then gather information about the concepts through laboratory activities. They next review the principles, rules or generalisations

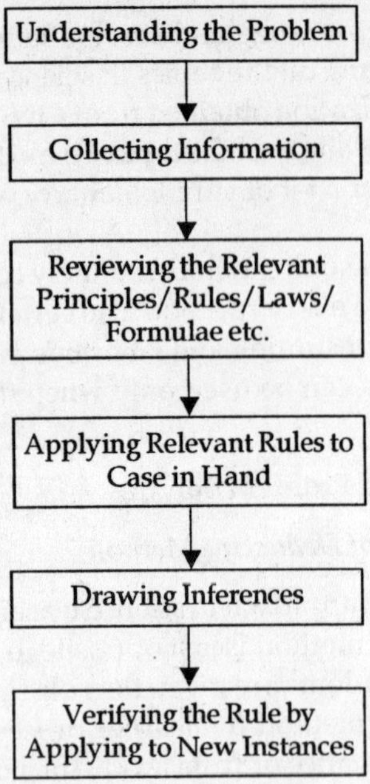


and identify the one that is best applicable to the problem. Inferences are drawn based on the application of the rule. The principle or rule on generalization is applied to the particular case. If it solves the problem then it is accepted; otherwise the procedure is repeated till a better solution is found.

The deductive approach is an effective way to reach a difficult content with difficult subject-matter, since all students may not be able to arrive at the rule or principle through the inductive approach. There is a possibility that a majority of students may respond to this method.

***Examples of Using Deductive Approach***

Let us think of a few instances where we can use this method

1. *Principle: Cooling is Caused by Evaporation*

Confirmation by Application numerous examples such as:

- Applying alcohol on one's hand.
- Observing feeling after taking a hot water bath.
- Water kept in earthen pots.

- Use of wet mats over windows etc.

2. *Verify the Formula for Finding the Focal Length of a Lens*
   $f = 1/4\,(d - x2/d)$

The students understand the terms involved as:

- f = focal length of lens
- d = distance of screen from source of light
- x = distance of lens from source of light.

The students adjust the position of lens to obtain sharp image on the screen without changing the position of source and screen and apply the rule in each case and verify it.

### *Advantages of Deductive Method*

We shall now try to list the merits of the Deductive method

*(i)* It is short and time saving method and hence is preferred by teachers. It is suitable for all classes.

*(ii)* It glorifies memory because students are required to memorise a large number of laws, formulae etc.

*(iii)* It is adequate and advantageous method for the revision of a topic.

*(iv)* It supplements inductive method and thus completes the inductive-deductive method of problem solving.

*(v)* It enhances speed and efficiency in solving numerical problems.

### *Limitations of Deductive Method*

Shall we now see what the limitations of this method are? They are:

*(i)* It is not a scientific method because the approach of this method is confirmatory and not explanatory.

*(ii)* It encourages rote memory because pure deductive work requires some law, principle, formula for every type of problem and it demands blind memorization of a large number of such laws and formulae etc.

*(iii)* In this method students are not completely active. It doesn't develop thinking, reasoning or discovery.

### Comparison between Inductive and Deductive Approaches

We shall now try to compare inductive and deductive approaches to problem solving:

| | *Inductive Method* | *Deductive Method* |
|---|---|---|
| 1. | One proceeds from specific to General | One proceeds from general to specific. |
| 2. | It is a psychological method with the student's nature as the nucleus | The stress here is on acquisition of facts. |
| 3. | It is a scientific method stimulating reflective thinking | This is not a discovery method. |
| 4. | Reasoning is the keynote in this approach | The stress is on rote memory. |
| 5. | This is suited for primary classes as it provides for direct and concrete experiences | It is better suited for high school classes. |
| 6. | This method is a time consuming process | It is an economical method in terms of time. It gives essential speed, skill and efficiency to problem solving. |
| 7. | The student is a very active participant | In this method the student is rather a passive participant. |

## CHOICE OF METHOD

### Introduction

As a physical science teacher uses a variety of methods and techniques for daily teaching. While choosing a method, we should assess its advantages and disadvantages in relation to others and also correlate the correct method with the objectives of education and the specific conditions in which learning takes place. In general, there is an interaction between teacher and the learner. To enhance this interaction, we science teachers tend to use new instructional materials.

### Factors to be Considered in the Selection of Methods

The criteria for selection of teaching methods are manifold. However, the most important factors are:

*(i)* human factors.
*(ii)* objectives of teaching.
*(iii)* time and materials available.
*(iv)* maturity level of students.
*(v)* student strength etc.

method is likely to stimulate the process of learning,

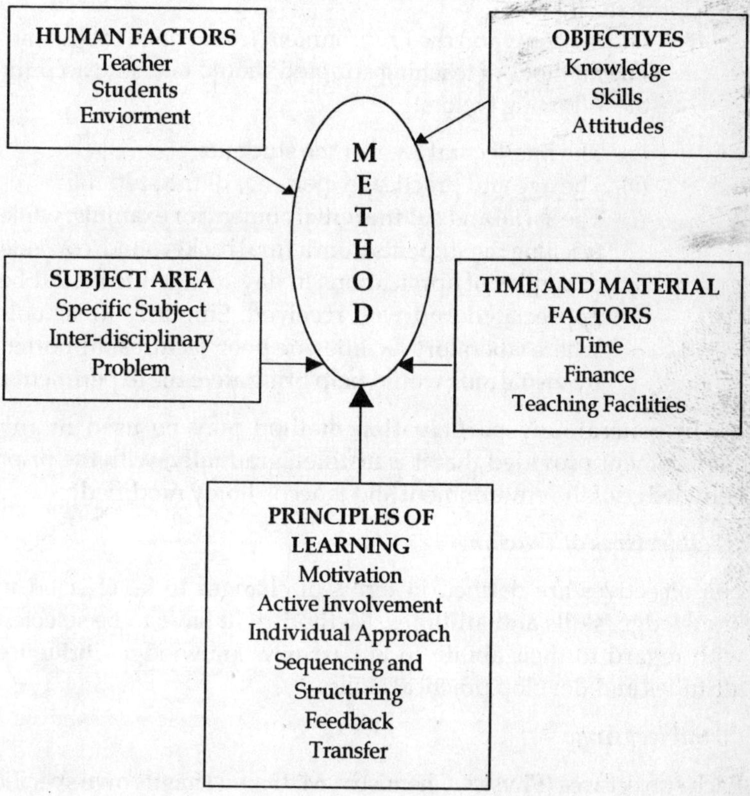


We shall represent the factors diagrammatically.

Shall we discuss each of the factors in detail?

**(1) *Human Factors***

The human factors that influence the selection of methods are: *(a)* teacher, *(b)* the students and *(c)* the environment from which they come.

- *The Teacher:* The knowledge, teaching experience and personality of the teacher are factors of primary importance. The teacher should have a clear and significant message to convey and a personality acceptable to the students for establishing effective communication links. If these conditions are fulfilled, a well chosen and properly used otherwise the method may be a failure and become an end in itself.

- The Students and the Environment from which they come: The methods of teaching adopted should take into account the following factors:
    - *(a)* The intellectual level of the students.
    - *(b)* The age and practical experience of the students.
    - *(c)* The social and cultural environment for example, while teaching the students from a rural background, concrete examples of applications in day-to-day life would be appreciated and well received. Similarly in schools where laboratory facilities are poor, lectures supported by visual aids would help bring alive the experiments.

In general, any participation method may be used in any environment provided that it is instilled gradually, with the prior knowledge of the environment and is accordingly modified.

***(2) Objectives of Teaching***

The objectives are defined in terms of changes to be effected in knowledge, skills and attitudes. Methods will have to be selected with regard to their ability to impart new knowledge, influence attitudes and develop practical skills.

***(3) Subject Area***

Each subject area (Physics, Chemistry, Maths, etc) has its own specific features. For example in physical chemistry, extensive use of mathematics is made. It could be taught through a combination of methods (using audio-visual aids) and numerical exercises during which the concepts could be mastered. The teacher should know 'when' to use which method and 'how'. It should be noted that is often possible to choose from several methods. Thus, a particular topic could be taught in different ways, using different methods by different teachers.

***(4) Time and Material Factors***

Decision on the choice of teaching methods depends on time, financial measures and other factors preparation time varies for different teaching methods. The teaching facilities may be a limiting factor in some schools in small townships factors such as number of rooms available, accessibility to audio visual aids, laboratory facilities should be anticipated and the methods selected should conform to the specific needs.

***(5) Principles of Effective Learning***

Any educational process accomplishes its role only by creating situations favourable to learning and in which learning actually takes place. Of course, principles of learning are not put into effect through the teaching method alone. A few principles of learning relevant to teaching methods are discussed below:

*Motivation*

The motivation to learn is enhanced if the presentation of the teaching material is interesting and emphasises on applied values. To some extent this could be obtained even using a good lecture combined with use of visual aids. However, many participative methods are directly concerned with the application of theoretical knowledge to real life situations. The diverse ways in which they can be combined and sequenced can add to the joy of learning and minimise the fatigue.

*Active Involvement*

The principle of active involvement implies that deeper the involvement, the higher the motivation, the more the students retain and the better they are equipped to apply it.

*Individual Approach*

Individuals have different capabilities of learning, have personal styles of study and application. They should be subject to individual control of performance. The overall methods of teaching have to initiate not only 'work in groups' but also provide the opportunity for individual reading, thinking and knowledge gained. This can be done through.

- Compulsory individual assignments (e.g. reading, exercises, projects).
- Use of teaching aids for individual learning, like audio and video tapes, teaching machines, computer terminals accessible to individual students.
- The breaking down of projects into modules of assignments for each individual.

- Voluntary additional work for the gifted students.
- Different types of feedback are needed and have to be provided in learning.

They are:

(*a*) Feedback on the student's competence and behaviour.
(*b*) Feedback on the effectiveness of the teaching method in achieving the stated objectives.

The principle of transfer requires that education should help the student to transfer what he has learned, to live situations.

Keeping in view, the principles of learning, it is necessary to properly combine and sequence various teaching methods in order to secure the greatest impact on learning.

## GUIDING PRINCIPLES FOR SELECTING TEACHING METHODS

Shall we now discuss about the guiding principles while selecting a method of teaching? They are:

(*i*) Every method we use should be based on an understanding level of the students in our classrooms and not on an understanding of children we have read about.
(*ii*) Every method we use should be one which we thoroughly understand and believe will be successful with the pupils in our classroom and not merely one which we have heard is successful.
(*iii*) Every method we use should lead the pupils to a sense of achievement through interest and purpose.
(*iv*) Every method we use should stimulate the pupils to think and co-operate actively.
(*v*) Every method we use should be based on the realization that the word education is derived from a Latin word 'educo' which means "I bring up" or "I nourish". Education is a "bringing out" process and not a "putting in" one.

There are certain other vital instincts which stimulate the child to learn and through which the child acquires knowledge and skills. They are instincts of play, imitation, curiosity and competition. These are the instincts which are principally concerned with the educational development of the child and which we must consider when planning our methods of teaching science.

Our teaching method should be compatible to our objectives. Let us suppose our objectives are:

*(i)* To ensure that the students obtain the factual knowledge of the subject.
*(ii)* To give the students an understanding of the basic concepts
*(iii)* To help the students acquire practical laboratory skills.
*(iv)* To promote the interest of students in the subject.
*(v)* To develop the students ability to communicate his understanding of the subject in their own words.

If we look at these objectives and choose suitable methods to achieve these objectives we may choose "lecture method" in order to achieve objectives

*(i)* and
*(ii)* But by lecture method we will not be able to achieve objectives.
*(iii)* and
*(iv)* for which perhaps the laboratory method would be more suitable. The lecture-demonstration method will be suitable to achieve objective.
*(v)* in which students take down their own notes.

Besides these vital instincts from which the impulse to learn springs, there are some physical agents which enable a child to acquire skills and knowledge. They are:

*(i)* The hands – learning by touching and doing
*(ii)* The eyes – learning by seeing
*(iii)* The ears – learning by hearing
*(iv)* The mouth – learning by saying
*(v)* The nose – learning by smelling
*(vi)* The tongue – learning by tasting.

These senses should be utilised as much as possible in our methods of physical science teaching for creating effective teaching learning situations.

**Selection of Teaching Method**

In the preceding five units we have thoroughly discussed various methods of teaching science. Each teaching method is unique. Different teaching methods are not just a matter of fashion or personal choice. A teaching method may prove to be suitable for one situation but completely inap propriate for another. As we have experienced the method that we adopt in any particular class will depend upon factors such as interests, our abilities, abilities of students, resources available, time constraints, etc. Each method has got its own merits and limitations. Students also differ and learn differently and hence require different methods to optimise learning. Hence, it is imperative that we are aware of all the methods and we should be able to choose the correct method i.e., choose the right method for the right job.

# 6

# The Year Plan, Unit Plan and Lesson Plan

## Introduction

Planning is a major requisite for all successful teaching. You must plan to become completely familiar with the science content pertinent to the topic being studied. You should also look for a variety of appropriate learning activities and develop desirable behavioural outcomes in your pupils. There should also be provision for evaluating the learning that takes place.

Hence, in this unit we describe the different levels of planning – the Year Plan and the Unit Plan. We also discuss in detail the steps in developing a year plan and a unit plan.

We hope that you would learn to plan your teaching interestingly and become efficient teachers.

## THE YEAR PLAN

The most general type of planning you will do as a classroom teacher is the year planning. In this long range plan, you lay out your instruction for the year.

While planning for the year, you have to consider the following factors:

- The number of units to be taught in the subject;
- The objectives to be realized through the various units;
- The number of periods available during the year;
- The number of periods to be assigned for testing.

**1. Formation of Units**

As a teacher you are expected to divide the content of your physical sciences textbook into suitable units.

**2. The Objectives to be Realized**

In every unit of a subject objectives related to knowledge, understanding, application and skills can be developed. Again through almost all units, interest, attitudes and appreciation can more or less be developed. You have to allot the number of periods for each unit depending on the weightage of the objectives to be realised.

**3. Time Available (for Teaching)**

You (as a teacher) should use your discretion and past experience while allotting adequate number of periods to the different units of a subject.

*Note:* The total number of periods available for instruction for Physical Science is 75 to 80, approximately.

**4. Time Required (for Testing)**

The number of periods required for unit testing and assignment should be indicated. Normally, in many secondary schools, the number of unit tests conducted is 4.

**Steps in the Year Plan**

***Step—I***

Divide the content in to units and sub-units.

***Step—II***

1. Allot the number of periods for each unit, depending on the scope and extent of the content to be taught.
2. Give weightage to the objectives to be realised.
3. Plan for practical activities involved in the unit.

***The Year Plan Performa***

School: Total number of periods:
Class: Subject:

## THE UNIT PLAN

You, as a teacher, must plan for a complete unit of work, with definite scope and sequence.

| *Sl. No.* | *Month & Year* | *Units* | *No. of Periods* | *Objectives* | | | | | | | *Methods of Teaching* | *Teaching Learning Material* | *Evaluation* |
|---|---|---|---|---|---|---|---|---|---|---|---|---|---|
| | | | | *K* | *U* | *A* | *S* | *I* | *AT* | *AP* | | | |
| | | | | | | | | | | | | | |

The elements of good planning have to be organised into a frame work.

**The Unit (Definition)**

The unit is a logical division of the class work or activity. The unit presents a plan for providing teaching learning activities that will achieve the objectives of the unit. "A unit is a large block of related subject matter as can be overviewed by the learner."

***Criteria of a Good Unit***

- A unit should keep in view the needs, abilities and the interests of the pupils.
- It should permit a variety of field trips, experiments, demonstrations and projects etc.
- It should take into account the previous experiences and background of the pupils.
- It should provide for new experiences.
- It must be flexible enough to permit digression at any point.
- It should be related to the social and physical environment of the pupils.
- It should be a part of a sequence that permits growth from year to year.

***Components of a Unit***

What does a unit contain? A unit should contain most—if not all—of the following:

- Overview;
- Objectives;
- Learning activities;
- Materials;
- Bibliography;
- New science vocabulary;

- Culminating activities;
- Work sheets.

Now, we will discuss each of the above components of a unit.

**1. *Overview***

The purpose of the overview is to describe the nature and scope of the unit:

One way of presenting an overview is to give it in the form of 2 or 3 paragraphs. You may begin the first paragraph by describing the importance of the unit topic in our daily lives.

Then, you can list the key concepts.

You may conclude by giving some general values and desirable behaviours the pupils will acquire from the unit.

Otherwise you can list the key concepts to be learned, followed by the desirable behaviours.

**2. *Objectives***

In general, as a science teacher, you have two main objectives.

1. to help the pupil learn the science content – the products of science;
2. to learn the processes of science – hence you have to incorporate both the objectives into the unit.

The second objective is realised by the development of desirable behaviours in the pupil such as, the science skills, attitudes, appreciations, thinking critically and creatively and solving problems.

**3. *Learning Activities***

These are the means by which the pupil learns both the content and the processes of science. As a classroom teacher, you can use a variety of learning activities such as,

- experiments;
- demonstrations;
- discussion, oral and written reports, films, observations and so forth.

You may use as many activities as are necessary to ensure satisfactory learning.

**4. *Materials, Bibliography, New Science Vocabulary***

Units usually list down the new vocabulary and all the materials needed for the learning activities. They should contain a bibliography of the textbooks and other reference materials that will be used during the unit.

**5. *Culminating Activities***

A culminating activity is an activity that concludes the unit. This helps summarize the learning and brings the objectives of the unit into focus.

**6. *Evaluation***

The unit can include the kinds of evaluation techniques that are used while the unit is in progress.

*Work Sheets*

You can present the working period in the form of a work-sheet either in a Single-running column: (in which the components of the unit are written in the form of running matter) or Parallel columns: (where the unit components are placed in a number of parallel columns).

*Kinds of Units*

These days the term unit is used loosely to describe any kind of teaching – learning situation. There are many kinds of units. However, many are quite similar. They differ a little either in their format or style. All units can be classified into three basic kinds.

1. Resource Units
2. Teaching Units and
3. Textbook Units

**1. *Resource Unit***

The study plan for a broad area of learning is known as a resource unit:

1. It consists of an extensive collection of objectives, activities and materials dealing with a science topic.
2. It is more comprehensive. It contains many more suggestions for study than any single classroom can pursue.

From the resource unit you, as a teacher, can select the learning activities that will best fit the needs and abilities of your pupils from.

1. It is organised in a broad and flexible fashion.
2. It includes the material that can be used for average, slow, and talented learners.

**2. *Teaching Unit***

A teaching unit constitutes the actual materials used and taught.

It is a detailed plan for teaching and learning in the classroom.

**3. *Textbook Units***

You know that the textbook units are developed around a nucleus of key concepts and conceptual schemes.

To prepare a textbook unit, follow these steps
first, construct an outline of science concepts for the unit.
Organise the concepts into a logical sequence;
Look for a variety of learning activities;

Make a list of the materials required. When completed, the textbook units become similar to the teaching unit.

**The Unit Plan**

The planning for a unit is known as the Unit Plan. While planning the unit, you must bear the following factors in mind:

- Objectives and specifications of the unit;
- Content analysis;
- Learning activities;
- Teaching learning materials;
- Testing procedures.

**Successive Steps in Unit Planning**

Before you make an attempt to develop a unit plan, you should be thoroughly familiar with the content of the unit. First, divide the unit into a number of sub-units. You may follow the following proforma initially for the schedule of work.

After, planning the schedule of work, you try to do the content analysis.

**Schedule of Work**

| *Sl. No.* | *Items Included in the Sub-unit* | *No. of Periods Class Periods* | *Lab – periods* |
|---|---|---|---|
| Sub-unit I | | | |
| Sub-unit II | | | |

## Content Analysis

To plan the unit, you have to analyse its content in to terms, concepts, facts, principles, relationships etc. This helps you to have a thorough knowledge of the subject matter and to teach with full awareness of the depth of the content:

Before you do the content analysis, read the content of the unit and while reading, underline the terms, principles, concepts etc., at relevant places and then prepare a list.

For example for the sub-unit-I, "Production and propagation of sound" from the unit 'sound' of class X, the content may be analysed in the following manner:

**Unit–X: Sound Sub-Unit – Production and Propagation of Sound Terms**

***Wave Motion***

Wave motion is a method of energy transfer in which the energy is transferred.

When a disturbance is caused in particulars of an elastic medium it is transferred from particle to particle and this is called wave motion.

***Wavelength : (x)***

This is the distance between successive crests, troughs or identical parts, of a wave.

***Frequency (n)***

This is the number of waves that pass a particular point per unit time.

***Wave Velocity (v)***

It is the speed with which waves pass by a particular point ( $v = n\underline{x}$)

***Transverse Wave***

A wave in which the particles of the medium vibrate in the direction perpendicular to the direction of wave propagation, is called a transverse wave.

***Longitudinal Wave***

When the particles of the medium execute vibrations in the direction of the wave, the waves are called longitudinal waves.

**Formulae**

V = nx
Vel = fre. wave length
n = 1/T = (where T is the period of vibration)
x = VT

**UNITS**

**Herts**

*(Cycle/Sec)*: The unit of frequency is called Herts (H) after Hdeinrich Herts, who discovered the radio waves in 1886.

Example of Transverse Waves:

Waves in the stretched strings of musical instruments and upon the surface of liquids are transverse; so also are C.M. waves, radio waves, visible light, x rays and so forth.

**STEP–I**

**Objectives – Specifications**

List out the objectives with specifications that can be realised through the content analysis.

You may differentiate the objectives in terms of cognitive, affective or psychomotor domains.

You are well-aware that

The Cognitive domain includes the objectives that invoke recall or recognition of scientific information.

The Affective domain relates to attitudes, interests, values and appreciations.

The Psychomotor domain constitutes the manipulation of motor skills and the lab-skills.

You may also list a combination of these domains without specific reference to the classification. To serve as a guideline for you, the objectives of teaching the sub-unit production propagation of sound are given below:

**General Objectives**

To understand that waves are a means of energy transfer. To study the production and nature of transverse and longitudinal waves.

To develop an understanding of the properties and characteristics of sound waves.

To understand that vibrations cause sound.

**STEP–II**

**Teaching-Learning Activities**

The third step is to organise those activities that will best achieve the specifications. You, as a teacher, should try to give different types of activities as

**1.** ***Initiating Activities***

For example, when you want to introduce the unit, Electro-magnetism.

You can take devices like the bell, buzzer, telegraph, motor etc., and ask the pupils to locate the electromagnet. Also ask, "How does the electromagnet work in each device?

**2.** ***Learning Activities***

While teaching the same unit, you may plan this activity.

Sprinkle some iron filings on a piece of white cardboard. Rest a coil of wire carrying current on the cardboard and tap the edge of the board and ask, What happened to the iron filings? What do you infer from this activity?

**3.** ***Enrichment Activities***

For the same unit, you can show how the following work:

- The Electric buzzer;
- The Electric bell;
- The Telephone transmitter and receiver;

- The Generator;
- Ask the pupils to make a simple;
- electric bell;
- You may also plan;
- possible experiments and/or Demonstrations;
- Discussion questions; and
- Practical activities to be done by pupils in the class as a class assignment.

### STEP–III

**Teaching - Learning Material**

Prepare a checklist of materials needed for each activity.

### STEP–IV

**Evaluation**

Include questions of categories such as,

- Class assignments;
- Assignment of activity type to be done by each pupil; and
- Practice type of assignment.

**Proforma of a Unit Plan**

Class: Name of the Unit:

Key concepts: Major objectives of the unit:

| *Sl. No.* | *Month & Year* | *Units* | *No. of Periods* | *Objectives* | | | | | | | *Methods of Teaching* | *Teaching Learning Material* | *Evaluation* |
|---|---|---|---|---|---|---|---|---|---|---|---|---|---|
| | | | | K | U | A | S | I | AT | AP | | | |
| | | | | | | | | | | | | | |

### LESSION PLAN

As a teacher in the class, before the pupils,

- do you want to avoid fumbling?
- be secure?
- be automatic in your delivery?
- avoid your lessons becoming stale and routine?
- Master the lesson content and related teaching skills?

If yes – you have to carefully plan each daily lesson.

The daily lesson plans can be vital to both the experienced and the beginner science teachers in improving their efficiency in teaching science.

Writing the Lesson Plan brings into focus the purpose, the content and the procedure to be followed:

**What is a Lesson?**

A lesson consists of the content to be taught and the instructional strategy employed in teaching of that content.

Instructional strategy = Method + Procedure (an outline to implementing the lesson).

**What is a Lesson Plan?**

A lesson plan in the words of B. Standa, "Is actually a plan of action. It is a classroom guide for the teacher as a visualisation of the classroom experiences he desires to occur; and is a guide to effective teaching."

**Why Lesson Planning?**

1. It keeps the teacher to be systematic and orderly in the treatment of the subject matter.
2. It prevents waste of time.
3. It gives confidence to the teacher.
4. It helps in effective teaching.

**Features of a Lesson Plan**

A lesson plan must help to clarify to the teacher the specific learning outcomes in pupils, in relation to the topic and indicate how these are proposed to be organised and evaluated. Regardless of the format of the plan, the lesson plan should contain the following features/ essential components:

1 . Objectives; Why teach this lesson?
Outline of the content ; What to teach in this lesson?
Methods; How to teach this lesson?
Evaluation; How do I know what I taught?

*Note:* You please recall the taxonomy of educational objective: 3 domains and the objectives specifications.

## Objectives

You have to list the objectives in terms of the development of pupil understandings, factual information, problem solving skills, scientific attitudes and developing new interests. You cannot attempt objectives covering all categories in one lesson. Some of these objectives are attained only over a long period of time.

For example, for a topic on "The gas laws" you may list down the following objectives:

1. to develop an understanding of Charles and Boyle's laws.
2. to develop skills in solving problems pertaining to the gas.
3. to develop the attitude and habit of verifying, accuracy in measurement and calculations.

If you list these three objectives for this lesson, you will select the appropriate content and method of teaching to develop them. For example, if skill in solving problem is to be emphasized, you should give opportunity to the pupils to solve problems.

Similarly, if you want to develop the skill in measurement and verification of the laws, you have to plan suitable activities/ demonstrations. Hence, the content and the procedure and learning activities for instruction must be appropriate to the objectives listed.

In block II, you have studied about the instructional objectives and specifications. A list of institutional objective specifications for a topic was also given there.

Using that knowledge, you have to first list down the instructional objectives and specifications for the lesson you are going to teach.

However, for further reinforcement, we have given below a list of the objectives and specifications for the lesson "Production and Propagation of Sound."

Name of the Topic : 'Production and Propagation of Sound'.

**Objectives and Specifications**

*Knowledge*

1. Recalls the terms like – wavelength, frequency, velocity of the wave, transverse wave, longitudinal wave.

2. Recognises the waves in the ripple tank (Transverse and longitudinal waves.)

***Understanding***

Distinguishes between a longitudinal and transverse wave.

1. Sees relationship between v, and n
2. Expresses correct units for the like x, v, -n
3. Gives examples of

– transverse waves and
– musical instruments which produce sound by vibrations.

***Applications***

The pupil predicts that vibrations are necessary for the production of sound.

The pupil infers that sound cannot travel in vacuum.

The pupil gives scientific reasons as to why bats can hear sounds of greater frequencies.

Why sound cannot travel in vacuum.

***Skill***

The pupil draws the sketches, latitudinal waves and train waves.

He draws sketches: Draws the diagram to show that sound does not travel in vacuum. He labels the diagram correctly.

***Content***

You have to select an outline of the content carefully in terms of objectives. The nature of the content should also reflect the kind of learning activities that the pupils will experience.

***Some Tips***

You have to take up only that much content, which you feel, you will be able to cover during a period of 40-45 minutes.

***Other Tips***

Encourage the pupils to bring in various supplementary material (like news articles, pictures, photographs etc), related/relevant to the topic.

Utilize all types of resource materials.
Never limit yourself to the textbook.

After selecting the content and the suitable materials for learning, you may analyse the content into various terms, facts, concepts etc.

*Note:* Please refer to the "Content Analysis" of the lesson "Production and propagation of sound" given under the unit plan.

**Methods (How to Teach this Lesson)**

In block II you have studied about the various methods used for teaching of science. Now you have to choose the method/methods which best suits/suit your lesson.

The objectives, the nature of the content, personality of the teacher and the class as a whole are the factors that determine the selection of appropriate method for teaching the lesson.

**Evaluation (How Do I Know that I Taught)**

This part of the lesson plan helps you to determine as to what degree learning has occurred during the classroom period. You have to ask a number of objective based questions throughout the class, and the pupil responses for your questions will help you to evaluate the extent of learning.

In addition to the questions and the pupils' oral responses, you can observe the pupils as they solve some problems in their seats. When you demonstrate an experience or when the pupils are involved in some group practical work, a careful observation of their work habits will also reveal the nature of their learning. As a teacher, you have to observe the pupil's error at the board, or at the desk, or during an experiment, and correct the mistake promptly. By this, you can prevent the blocks in learning the major ideas of the lesson.

**Steps in a Lesson Plan**

There are many types of lesson plan. Herbart and other educators have emphasized the following six steps:

***Hebartion Steps***

- Preparation or Introduction;
- Presentation;
- Comparison or Association;
- Generalisation;

- Application;
- Recapitulation.

Though Herbart suggested 6 steps, we, in the colleges of Education, club some of the above steps and emphasize only on the following steps while training the student-teachers in preparing their lessons.

Let us discuss these steps of lesson planning in detail.

**Introduction and Motivation**

The pupil should be in a receptive frame of mind before you start teaching. You have to arouse curiosity in the pupils and create a desire in the pupils to take part in the lesson courteously. You greet the pupils. Be friendly and sociable, and then introduce the present lesson.

You might motivate them by

1. Asking a number of provocative questions.
2. Stating objectives to the pupils—like by explaining to them what they will be able to learn by the end of the lesson unit.
3. Explaining the personal importance of the lesson to the pupils like what they can become if they learn this lesson etc.

There are various ways of introducing the lesson and it requires a skill on the part of the teacher to introduce a lesson.

The skills of introducing a lesson involves the use of various techniques and devices. They are:

- Testing previous knowledge of the pupils.
- Using appropriate devices.

***(1) Testing Previous Knowledge of the Pupils***

Educationally, it is vital to proceed from known to unknown. This can be achieved by testing the pupil's previous knowledge gained in the previous lesson or from daily experiences. You have to link up the background knowledge with the new knowledge.

However, the questions you ask to test their previous knowledge should be related and relevant to the new topic you present.

*For example:* If you want to teach a lesson on "Chemical bonding", you have to ascertain their previous knowledge, by asking questions related to Atomic number, Atomic weight; Electronic configuration etc. Unless the pupil knows these things you cannot teach the present topic on hand. Therefore, you have to carefully establish the knowledge that is required to follow the present lesson.

***(2) Using Appropriate Device***

The device refers to the technique that the teacher uses while introducing a lesson. Such a device can be:

- Use of examples/analogies/similarities etc.
- Questioning.
- Describing/narrating/story telling.
- Use of A.V. Aids.
- Experimentation/demonstration.

(a) *Using examples etc.:* You can introduce a lesson by eliciting/ giving a number of examples leading to a principle, law, phenomenon or some concept.

(b) *Questioning:* The art of questioning is critical while teaching a lesson. We ask questions to obtain feed back about the level of understanding in the class:
- Promote thinking;
- draw attention ;
- to find opportunities to praise and encourage a student.
- and to provide the pupil an opportunity to verbalize his ideas in a coherent manner.

(c) *Describing/Narrating/Story Telling:* Sometimes, narration of some interesting instances or stories will create interest in the subject to be taught.

(d) *Use of A.V. Aids:* The use of A.V. aids secures the pupil's attention more quickly than any other device. You can use nice transparencies with OHP and project some slides on film strips.
You can also show beautiful photographs/pictures of rare things like glaciers-geysers etc.

(e) *Experimentation /Demonstration:* You may introduce many lessons in Physics/Chemistry with an interesting Demonstration/experiment.

*For example:* To introduce "Bernouli's principle" You may take a sheet of paper, just blow air across the lower surface of the paper, ask the pupils to observe what happens, question why it happens – explain and declare the topic. However, your introduction should be brief and interesting and in any case should not take more than 5 minutes.

(*f*) *Presentation:* This is the stage of actual presentation of the subject matter. By this stage, the teacher and the pupils should be engaged upon a common pursuit.

The teacher should engage himself in appropriate activities such as demonstrating, questioning, supervising, developing blackboard work. Simultaneously evaluating and also providing activities to the pupils such as observing, taking notes of the salient features, helping in demonstrations etc., can also be undertaken.

For presenting the subject matter you have to make use of the knowledge of the various methods you have studied earlier.

In teaching physical sciences, you may use a blend of the inductive and the deductive methods you have studied earlier. You may use suitable aids to make the lesson more interesting and comprehensive. You may also provide a variety of learning experiences for the pupils.

**Blackboard Work/B.B. Summary**

It is essential to develop a neat outline of the content presented on the Blackboard as it helps in better retention of the points by the pupils.

Here are a few precautions to be borne in mind while using the blackboard.

1. Write only the salient points one after the other as they are being developed.
2. The points written on the B.B., should have continuity (one linked logically with the previous one) in them.
3. The B.B. summary should be brief and simple so that the pupils can recollect the whole lesson at a glance.
   - Use coloured chalks sparingly to bring about contrast.
   - Draw simple, large and clear illustrations and diagrams.
   - Retain only relevant matter, rub off-unnecessary details.

**Recapitulation (Revision and Conclusion)**

Revising and reinforcing the salient points of the lesson is essential for any piece of teaching. Without this even the best presentation will only be partically successful. It is vital to conclude the lesson with an emphatic summary of what has been taught.

Therefore, allocate the last five minutes for a systematic review and recapitulation of what is taught by asking relevant, objective based questions. This enables you to find out whether the pupils have followed what has been taught and whether the method of teaching is effective.

**Home Assignment and Follow-up Activities**

The teacher has to give some questions for the pupils to be answered at home and also suggest some activities which could be done at home.

*Format of the Lesson:* The format of the lesson plan contains the following items:

Steps:

- Teaching items (content) ;
- Objectives and specifications;
- Teacher activity;
- Pupil activity;
- Teaching learning materials;
- Blackboard work.

**Proforma for a Lesson Plan**

Preliminaries

**Instructional Objectives and Specifications Content Analysis**

PROFORMA

| *Content* | *Objectives/ Specifications* | *Teacher Activity* | *Student Activity* | *Blackboard Work/ Teaching-Learning Material* | *Evaluation* |
|---|---|---|---|---|---|
| | | | | | |

1. Motivation
2. Introduction
3. Declaration
4. Presentation
5. Recapitulation
6. Home-work and follow-up Activity.

**Observation and Criticism of a Lesson**

The various areas, and the points that have to be carefully observed and against which constructive suggestions have to be offered are given below in the form of a proforma:

**Criticism Notes by Teacher Whose Lesson is Criticised**

| | |
|---|---|
| Class: | Time : |
| Strength of pupils in the Class: | School: |

**Items of Observation**

**I. *The Lesson***

1. What it aims at?
2. Introduction
3. Adequacy of the content presented
4. Suitability of method adopted
5. Extent of application brought in
6. Recapitulation
7. Assignment.

**II. *Teaching Aids and Devices***

1. Illustrations;
2. Models and specimens;
3. Experiments;
4. Student's work;
5. B.B.Work.

**III. *The Teacher***

1. Preparation of equipment etc.
2. Questions;
3. Language;
4. Voice and tone;
5. Self-confidence;
6. Activity and tact;

7. Reaction to student's response;
8. Discipline.

IV. *The Class*

1. Attention and interest;
2. Responses;
3. Co-operation;
4. Self-Discipline.

V. *Conclusion*

1. How far the objectives were achieved?
2. Whether the lesson was completed in time?
3. Causes for success or failure of 'the lesson'.
4. Suggestions for improvement.
5. Supervisor's remarks.

**Learning Experiences**

Many attempts have been made to define learning but so far no one has been able to give an accepted and adequate definition of learning. However, it is much easier to describe and explain what takes place in human learning. There has always been a general agreement among various authorities on the subject that learning refers to a more of less permanent change in behaviour, hitch occurs as a result of practice, the permanent change in behaviour is learning.

Thus, acquiring knowledge, broadening of understanding, improvement in physical skills, developing of attitudes, deepings of appreciation, etc., are classified as changes in behaviour.

Learning is an inferred process, for one can never observe it directly. Suppose a teacher teaches a theorem. After the teaching is over, he says that he has taught the theorem. Can a student say that he has learnt it? There is no evidence that he has. How then, is the teacher to know that the student has learnt the theorem? He has to put a test.

It is only from the student's performance that the teacher judges the changes in performance that has taken place before and after he has introduced the theorem. This change in performance (i.e., reaction or response) indicates the occurrence of learning.

## Learning Activities and Learning Experiences

The term learning activities may be explained as activities, which include an arrangement of teaching aids, questioning, explanation, observations, visits, handling of apparatus, models charts and specimen etc., reading, writing, drawing, etc. and which ultimately lead the students to learning.

Providing learning activities in the class or even outside of it is known as teaching. Listening to teachers, listening to students, speaking, thinking, observing, recalling, drawing, figures, locating places on a man, etc. are learning activities. The classroom teacher provides these activities to his students. This is known as teacher's teaching.

## Learning Experiences

Children learn by felling, thinking and acting. Learning results from the active participation of the children in the stimulus situation, which the teacher provides in the class. Learning experience is an interaction of the learner and the situation provided by the teacher. Each of these learning experiences modifies the behaviour of the pupil.

When a student takes part in learning activities, he develops certain understandings he realizes, feels, and appreciates some thing. As a result of learning activity, the student gets some after – effects in the form of understanding or realization or feeling or appreciation. These after – effects are called learning experiences. These learning experiences depend upon how well the teacher organizes learning activities. The more adequate and methodical the learning activities are, the richer will be the learning experiences.

In order to produce different types of learning experiences, the teacher may provide various activities, if he provides different learning activities, different types of learning experiences will result. Again, in order to produce a particular type of learning experience, a variety of learning activities may have to be provided for.

## Classification of Learning Experiences

Learning experiences can be classified into two categories:

*(a)* Direct Experiences; and
*(b)* Indirect Experiences.

***(a) Direct Experiences***

First hand experiences with various objects or symbols are termed "Direct Experiences." These experiences are more than perceptual learning in the sense that they include experiences with symbols. Perceptual learning arises out of experiences dependent upon seeing, hearing, smelling, tasting, touching, feeling, handling and manipulating objects in various ways. We get the meanings of terms like sweet—sour, hard, green coloured, pulling, pushing etc. through perceptual learning. We use symbolic words to describe them. Some of the illustrations of direct experiences are given below:

- Observing the objects, sample, models etc.
- Experimenting with physical and chemical materials.
- Setting up of apparatus for experiments.
- Constructing models, charts, plans, diagrams etc.
- Drawing figures, painting models.
- Dramatizing historical events.
- Summarizing a lengthy description.
- Collecting, analyzing and interpreting the data and generalizing them.
- Listing the important facts, points.
- Presenting ideas orally or in writing.

***(b) Indirect Experiences***

Those experiences, which are not first hand experiences, are terms as "Indirect Experiences." In this case, the direct experiences of others are made use of. It is very difficult to have direct experiences in all matters. Every student cannot get a direct experience in matters such as tremors of an earthquake, feelings while travelling by air or by sea, etc. A student can appreciate them through imagination only. Indirect learning experiences also have a place in the process of learning. A student reading the description of the Mount Everest will be thrilled. Even in the absence of the object or the stimulus (here, the Mount Everest), a student will have a thrilling experience, which, is an indirect experience. Some examples of indirect experiences are:

- Reading information or descriptions or discussions in books, magazines, journals, newspapers, etc.
- Observing pictures, photos, maps, models, etc.
- Listening to oral descriptions, lectures, talks, etc.

It may be pointed out here that it is rather difficult to completely separate the activities resulting in direct and indirect experiences; it may not even be desirable to do so. In many activities there may be combinations of direct and indirect experiences.

### Characteristics of Good Learning Experiences

The responsibility of the classroom teacher is to provide to his students learning situations composed of a variety of learning activities, so that they may have direct as well as indirect learning experiences, which ultimately result in learning.

1. The learning experiences should be directly related to the behavioural objectives, since our aim is to achieve the behavioural objectives through learning experiences.
2. The learning experiences should be meaningful. For example, asking the students to take down the information written on the blackboard without understanding it will not result in a meaningful experience.
3. The learning experiences should satisfy the psychological needs of the learner.
4. The learning experiences should be appropriate to the maturity level of the learner.
5. The learning experiences should be related to the life situations, so that they may be more effective, more meaningful and the learner will be more satisfied.
6. The learning experiences should be reinforced. Both types of reinforcements, positive and negative may be made use of in enriching the experiences.
7. The learning experiences should be intensive. The use of audio-visual aids would be very helpful in producing intensive experiences and changing the intensity of experiences.
8. The learning experiences should be varied, rich in content and novel. Multi–sensory experiences will be helpful in sustaining the interest in an activity.
9. The learning experiences should be related to the availability of the material and to the time.

### Source of Learning Experiences

A person lives amongst thousand of stimuli around him. In his conscious state, a person is always reacting to stimuli. He has a lot of chances to change his reactions (behaviour) in a desirable direction that is to learn. He has every chance of having learning experiences. There are many sources of learning experiences. They are:

1. *Home:* The home provides a number of learning experiences, e.g., talking, doing, walking, running etc. The home is mostly an informal agency.
2. *Society:* Many desirable and undesirable experiences are provided by society. Many devices and virtues are likely to be developed through all these experiences.
3. *Peer Groups:* Learning experiences through the peer groups help in developing such qualities as honesty, we – feeling, leadership, etc.
4. *School:* A school is a society in miniature. This is a formal agency providing a variety of learning experiences.
   (a) *Experiments:* They provide learning experiences related to laboratory skills.
   (b) *Excursions and Visits:* They provide learning experiences, which help students to develop certain good qualities like cooperation, association, helpfulness dignity of labour etc.
   (c) *Exhibitions:* They provide learning experiences, which help students to develop the skill of preparation and presentation, etc.
   (d) *Audio-visual Aids:* They widen the scope of knowledge and understanding. Again, they provide learning experiences, which develop pupil's interest.
   (e) *Co-curricular Activities:* Debating, elocution, dramatization, etc. help students to achieve skill in expression, systematizing arguments, reasoning, etc.
   (f) *Sport and Games:* They provide learning experiences, which help students to develop qualities like leadership, an attitude of cooperation, and an ability to follow others, we feeling, sportsmanship, etc.
   (g) *Methods of Teaching:* Group discussion method, assignment method, workshops, seminars, etc., provide various types of learning experiences to idem the horizon of the student's knowledge and understanding.
   (h) *School Library:* Books, journals magazines, etc., enrich the student's knowledge and understanding.
5. *Mass Media:* Radio, TV, newspapers, libraries, etc., enrich the knowledge and understanding of students.

# 7
# Science Laboratories

## Introduction

No course in Science can be considered as complete without including some practical work in it. Science laboratories are the places and means with the help of which all these necessary activities can be performed smoothly and effectively.

At school stage, practical work is every more important because of the fact that we 'learn by doing' scientific principles and applications thus rendered more meaningful.

The arrangement, setting and environment of the laboratory energize the students to perform their experiments carefully in a congenial atmosphere.

Laboratories are helpful in creating and promoting scientific attitude, sense of co-operation and spirit of healthy competition in the students.

## Planning of Science Laboratories

Before constructing the laboratory, the following factors should be taken into consideration at the planning stage:

1. The number of pupils working at a time.
2. The minimum space necessary for each pupil for comfortable working.
3. Number of science teachers in secondary schools.
4. Need for ancillary accommodation for storage.
5. Designing the science classroom and laboratory in such a

way that it could be used for science teaching both for middle school classes and for high school classes.

6. Imperative need for economy.

## Types of Science Laboratories

Keeping in view the further mentioned assume member of laboratory designs and their equipments have been suggested by different educationists. Some of the laboratories which suit the conditions of our country and which have been accepted by educationists are discussed here under.

### For High Schools

1. Lecture room-cum-laboratory plan by Dr. R.H. White house.
2. All-purpose laboratory.

### 1. *Lecture Room-cum-Laboratory Plan*

The plan was designed by Dr. R.H. White house, a former principal of the Central Training College, Lahore for high schools. It is economical and convenient for the teacher and the taught.

*Layout:* A room of 45′ × 25′ (13.5 mt × 7.5 mt) dimension, in which half of the part utilized for lecture-cum-demonstration work for 40 students and the rest for laboratory practical work for 20 students. The room should be facing north to facilitate proper amount of sunlight and fresh airflow.

*Walls:* Walls should be 11/2 (4.5 cm) thickness and atleast a height of 1mt painted the walls from the floor. The rent should be distempered.

*Air:* The floor should be slightly slanting to one side so that it can be washed with water easily. The flour should be cemented or tiled for cleanliness. There should be proper drainage.

*Doors:* There must be two doors, one near the lecture room and another near the laboratory. They should open outwards.

*Windows:* Three windows of 6′ × 8′ (1.8 mt × 2.4 mt) each should be placed opposite doors. One should be near the practical benches and two should be near the seating accommodation. There should be proper arrangement for window blinds and curtains on the doors. So that the room may be darkened for doing some light experiments when required.

*Seating Arrangement and Furniture:* In the area meant for lecture room a wall blackboard 10′ × 4′ (3 × 1.2 mt) is preceded. At a distance of 3′ (1 mt) from it is teacher's table 6′ × 2½′ (2 × 0.8 mt) high can be conveniently used both s writing table and a demonstration table.

Twenty dual tables and forty chairs are provided for the students. Dual tables should be of the size 3.5′ × 1.5′ × 2′ (105 × 45 × 60 cm) with the provision of shelf below. The chairs are 1.5′ (0.5 mt) high in the seat.

The area necessary for a dual table and two chairs is a square of 3.5′. Passages of 1.5′ are sufficient for single file and 2.5′ to 3.5′ at the sides.

A sink (18″ × 1″ × 6″ dimensions) is provided for the use of the teacher.

*Laboratory:* The laboratory room is with the provision of six laboratory tables (5 for the students and one for the teacher). These tables are of the size of 6′ × 3.5′ × 3 with the provision shelf below. A blackboard of 10′ × 4′ (3 × 1.25 mt) is also provided on this side of the room. Each table should have water connection with sink, an electrical connection and LPG gas connection.

In the Plan, there is a provision of 8 admirals (each with 7′× 5′ dimensions) with provision of 1.5′ deep shelves for storage of apparatus, equipment etc.

For chemicals, balances and articles, tables with 100 × 75 cm dimension can be placed between two windows near the wall.

***Advantages***

The Following are the advantages are having with the lecture room-cum-laboratory:

- It is very economical.
- It is compact and provides enough space for seating, working, storage etc.
- It can be furnished easily and with meagre resources.
- It provides seating and storage accommodation in the compact and restricted space.
- In this room science atmosphere prevails.

### All Purpose Laboratory

This laboratory serves the purpose of both practical as well as theoretical work, but it may not be possible to carry out an effective teaching of special subject with this type of laboratory.

The size of the laboratory can be varied according to the number of students in the class. The usual dimensions of 45′ × 25′ are sufficient for 40 pupils. Storage-cum-preparation room should be provided along with the laboratory. This will improve the efficiency of working and preserving of apparatus.

Provisions can be made in the wall for reagent, bottles etc., in such a way that it neither abstracts lights nor looks ugly. The windows may be fitted with good blinds so that the room may be darkened when need be.

The furnishing and fitting can be done as shown in the figure. It is advisable to use movable tables with flat top, so that the table can be used both for practical work and for writing purpose and can be placed against one another at certain occasions. The side benches may be provided with sinks, water and gas taps. It is better to have these side benches of widow-ledge height so that the things that require light, such as aquaria and vivaria may be placed on them. Cupboards may be provided under these benches for storage purposes. A space about 3′ should be left between the wall and the tables. Two blackboards of 10′ × 4′ may be provided on each side of the laboratory.

### Importance of Laboratory Work

Learning by doing is one of the cardinal principles of science teaching. The achievements of modern science are mainly due to the application of experimental method. It is therefore important that the practical work should form a prominent feature in any science course. The primary objective in determining a technique of instruction is to provide for a maximum of pupil activity.

These are the some of important values in experimental work.

- With the practical orientation, students can find the reality and they will be answer at any time.
- Increases the curiosity to handle things. Develops active participation in the practical work.

- Develops the scientific knowledge, attitude and interest among the students. Providing an enthusiastic experimenter and discover.
- Provides opportunities for training in scientific method. Students get a good deal of training in facing the problems in a scientific way.
- Impose the good qualities like co-operation, initiative, self-reliance, self-dependence, resourcefulness etc.,
- Provides opportunities to exercise reading scales and drawing diagrams and custom pupils to use various hard tools of the scientists.

**Administration of the Laboratory**

A science teacher must keep these points in mind while conducting the practical work (administrating a lab).

1. Arrange those experiments in the laboratory which he has taught in the class.
2. Develop interest and curiosity among the students towards practical work. There is no mechanical repetition of the same experiments given in the textbook; teacher may make some alterations and additions in order to arouse divergent thinking on the part of the pupils.
3. Assign the practical based on the physical and intellectual conditions of the students.
4. Explain clearly the aim, procedure and care take of the experiment to the students.
5. Prompt observation should be kept on all the students and if any student is in need of help provide the help to him.
6. He should see that the experiments must be completed and recorded by the student.
7. Correct the records or observation books of the students and give right suggestions if necessary.
8. According to the number of available equipments, time and number of students- planning the experiments either to do individually or in groups.
9. Place the things in an alphabetical order of the articles in the cupboards and drawers and paste a list of the articles on it. The same may be maintained in a record. It helps any one anything at to locate any time easily to any one.

10. Instruction must be given to the students to clean the apparatuses after these practical works or before replacing them.
11. Provide the laboratory manuals or instructional cards for students before going to perform the experiment. The manual or instructional card (6′ × 4′ dimension) clearly contains the name of the experiment, purpose, method, procedure, observations, precautions, and conclusions.
12. The teacher must display the laboratory rules inside and outside of the lab and the students should be asked to follow them strictly.
13. A list of precautions against fire, poisionable chemicals, electricity and other accidents should also be displayed. If possible orient the students about these accidents and the use of first aid kit.
14. Loose or obscure labels should be replaced by new ones.
15. Replace the outdated chemicals in the almirahs.
16. Provision must be given to the students in preparing the improvised and low cost apparatus.

## Maintaining of Laboratory Registers

Maintenance of a record of the apparatuses material etc., in the laboratory is one of the important duties of the science teacher. The following records/registers should be maintained in the laboratory.

### 1. *Order Register*

It is meant for orders sent for the purchase of new apparatus:

| *Sl.No.* | *Date of Order* | *Name of the Firm and Place* | *Details of Articles Ordered* | *Articles Revival* | *Cost* | *Signature* |
|---|---|---|---|---|---|---|
| | | | | | | |

For convenience a copy of the order is posted on the left hand page of this register and a copy of supply under be posted on the right hand page.

### 2. *Issue Register*

It is meant for issuing the articles to the students at the time of practical work or else and to others too.

| Sl.No. | *Name of the Student / Person* | *Date* | *Articles Name and Quality* | *Signature of the Student /Person* | *Signature Return on with Date* |
|---|---|---|---|---|---|
| | | | | | |

### 3. *Requirement Registers*

If maintaining this register the logic of placing order becomes easier. Teacher will enter the items whose absence is felt by the teacher at the time of demonstration of an experiment or during the practical class.

### 4. *Stock Registers*

They are four kinds.

(a) *Stock Register for Non-Breakable Articles:* Non-breakable articles and apparatus their qualities/cost etc., are entered in this register.

| Sl.No. | *Date* | *Company Name & Address* | *Name of the Article & Description* | *Rate* | *Quality* | *Total Cost* | *Remarks* | *Initial of the In-charge* |
|---|---|---|---|---|---|---|---|---|
| | | | | | | | | |

(b) *Stock Register for Breakable Articles:* In this, in the first instance, the breakables are entered in different categories. Then the articles and their number, broken from time-to-time must be shown.

(c) *Register for Consumable Articles:* In this chemicals/ compounds which are of daily use and consumptions are entered. Their consumption should also be shown regularly so that the balance is always determined and verified.
The above proform of the register applicable to this register also.

(d) *Stock Register for Science Club:* In this register all the apparatus meant for science club must be entered. Entries of improvised apparatus, models, charts and collections made by the students should also be made in this register.

| Sl. No. | Name of the Student Class and School Address | Articles | | | | Use of the Article | Date of Collection | Signature of the Student | Initial of the in-Charge |
|---|---|---|---|---|---|---|---|---|---|
| | | Chart | Model | Improvised Apparatus | Collection | | | | |
| | | | | | | | | | |

**Administration of Science Laboratories**

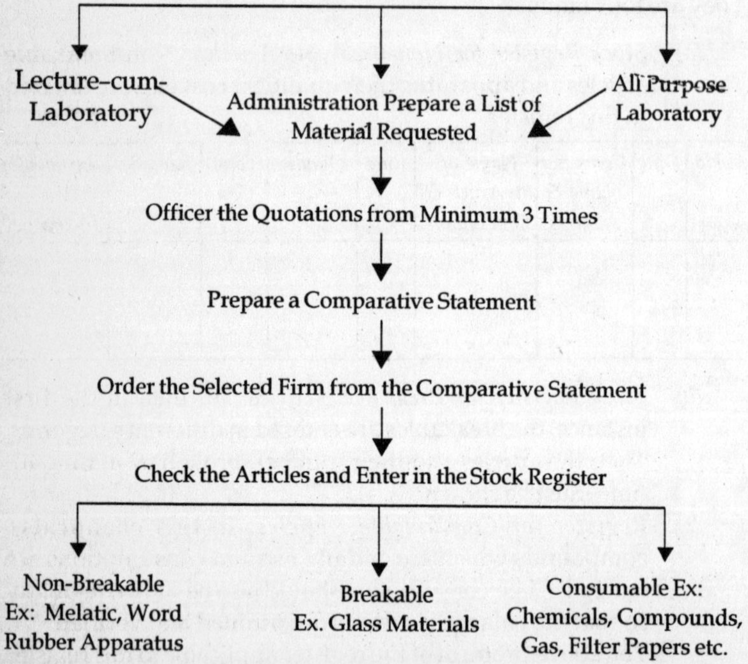


## Science Kits and Development of Low Cost Improvised Apparatus

### Science Kits

For the effective teaching of various topics in the subjects like physical and life sciences it becomes essential to demonstrate certain experiments. These experiments cab be performed if some minimum apparatus and material are provided. In India, all the schools are not have laboratory facilities. Even if they have, they will be with inadequate equipment and material. In order to make teaching of provide the science teaching effectively, the central science workshop in the NCERT has produce of science kits. "A box containing the minimum apparatus and material etc., required for experiments and demonstration are readily available to the teachers and students" is called science kit.

**Importance and Advantages of Science Kits**

The presently available science kits easy to carry from one place to another are generally called portable mini-laboratories. These kits are important for science teachers who are working in rural area schools and also for training the teachers in science in the remote areas.

Some of the advantages from the science kits are listed below:

1. It contains the apparatus for both physical and life sciences. It is an advantage for a teacher to demonstrate several experiments.
2. The kits have proved quite economical in the long run even with regard to the expenses incurred on consumable material.
3. The exact quantity of consumable material is indicated and therefore wastage is avoided.
4. Every kit has an instructional booklet for its use. The users get complete guidance for its handling.
5. The kits do not require extra source of energy like water supply, gas or electric supply for their use. Therefore, these can be conveniently used in rural areas and even in smaller towns.
6. It serves the students scientific hobbies because the apparatus in these kits are not cause any accidents.

**Types of Science Kits**

Department of Science Education and NCERT have also produced several kits, particularly for the primary and middle stage classes.

***Primary Science Kit***

It has been developed with primary objective of serving as a complete mini-laboratory for the science education in primary schools of our country specially covering the syllabus of III, IV and V classes designed by NCERT.

It is made of iron sheets; on stretching it can some as demonstration or laboratory table. It has a provision for a chalk board, display charts and pictures etc. There is also a tool box provided in this kit for undertaking the minor repairs and improvisation of the apparatus.

With the growing popularity of the kits a number of organisations and business firms have emerged in the market for the manufacturing of very useful kits. They have sought the permission from government and NCERT to prepare and sell these kits. Some of the kits developed by these firms are given below:

***Young Electrician***

With the help of this kit, 120 experiments related with the facts and principles of electricity can be performed. A guide book of 47 pages is given along with this kit.

***Young Optician and Photographer***

With the help of this kit, 120 experiments employing appropriate lenses mirrors and prisms etc., can be performed. A guide book of 60 pages is given along with this kit.

***Young Chemist***

With the help of this kit, 170 experiments related with the subject and world of chemistry can be performed by the students. There is a guide book of 58 pages available with this kit.

***Technical Child***

The children can perform 170 experiments with this kit in elementary physics on topics and contact related to water, air, steam etc. It also has an instructional booklet of 68 pages.

***First-Aid Box***

Accidents usually occur in the laboratory. So a first-aid kit should be kept in each laboratory in a separate cupboard. It is marked with a red cross (+) prominently. It must be kept in good condition and regularly inspected by the teacher.

"If any accident occurs to a person; before taking him to a doctor we are during some remedial clinic to him with the available medicines. A box contains these apparatus is called First-Aid Box." Its motto is "Prevention is better than Cure."

**Apparatus in the First-Aid Box**

1. All types and sizes of bandages
2. Surgical cotton
3. Adhesive plaster
4. Universal antidote
5. Germicide ointment
6. A pair of scissors
7. Safety pins
8. Eye both cup and dropper
9. Forceps
10. Surgical lint's
11. Penciline eye lotions and locula
12. Distilled water
13. Sarson oil, olive oil, glycerine
14. Boric acid, Tannic acid
15. Sodium bicarbonate, sodium carbonate
16. Burnol, vaseline
17. Tincture iodine
18. Hydrogen peroxide
19. Potassium permanganate
20. Clinical thermometer

**Common Accidents—Use of First-Aid Box**

*Fire*

Small fires due to oil, phosphorous, sodium etc., can be by extinguished by throwing some sodium bicarbonate or dry sand on them.

*Burns*

(*a*) For slight burns apply burnal and sarson oil. For small burns apply sterilized pad of cotton soaked in $NaHCo_3$ solution.

(*b*) Acid burns must be worked with clean water and wash with $NaHCo_3$ solution and apply finally some tannic acid.

(*c*) Alkali burns with 1 per cent of acetic acid solution or lemon juice or apply some Burnol.

(d) Phosphorus burns immerse in water and then treat with Dil. $AgNo_3$ solution.

***Eye Injuries***

In case of eye injuries, preliminary treatment can be given the patient before taking him to the doctor.

(a) If Acid falls in the eye, should be wash the eys with water and apply small quality of $NaHCo_3$ solution.
(b) If eye injury happened with alkalis, the eye with water and apply some boric acid solution.
(c) If solid substances injuries to the eye, clean the eye with wet surgical cotton or fine camel hair brush dipped in glycerin.

***Cuts***

It is easier to know whether a vein or an artery has been cut from the flow of the blood. If it is a continuous flow, then the vein has been injured and if it spurts then artery has been cut.

(a) The bleeding from minor cuts can be stopped by applying some pressure on the wound in the form of a dressing or applying some tincture Iodine on a pad of surgical cotton and placed on the wound.
(b) For serious cuts try to stop bleeding by applying pressure above the cut and rush to the hospital for treatment.

***Poisons***

In case of poisoning, medical advice should at once be sought.

(a) In case of solids, a spoonful of table salt in a tumbler of water should be given and encourage the patient to vomit.
(b) In case of Acids, much water followed by lime water or milk of magnesia.
(c) In case of caustic alkaline, dilute by drinking water and then drink a glass of lemon or orange juice.
(d) In case of Mercury compounds, immediately give one table spoonfull of salt or $ZnSo_4$ in a tumbler of warm water.
(e) In case of pungent gases like Chlorine, $So_2$, Bromine vapours etc., remove the victim to the open air and loosen the clothing at the neck. The patient should inhale dilute vapours of ammonia with $NaHCo_3$ solution.

## Low Cost Improvised Apparatus

As ours is a developing country, we have limited financial resources. Due to the financial constraints we require the production of improvised and inexpensive learning aids for imparting effective and efficient science education.

Improvisation in itself is a skill which must be learnt by every student. During improvisation, a lot of learning by thought and action processes takes place. Making improvised models and apparatus with readily available materials helps in satisfying the creative use of the students. Children are basically active by nature and they wish to use their hands for creating things and improvisation provides for achieving this end.

Simply it can be defined as "Those learning aids which are prepared from simple and readily available cheap material by students and teacher."

## Characteristics of Improvised Apparatus

The following are some of the characteristics of low cost Improvised apparatus:

1. The raw materials are easily available either free or at low cost in the local environment.
2. The materials do not involve specialized skills and can be made by pupils, teachers or members of the community.
3. The materials can be easily and effectively used by the teachers and pupils in clarifying the set objectives.
4. The process involved in the production of the materials is simple and inexpensive.
5. The material is simple, accurate and appropriate to the age level of the users.
6. The material stimulates thinking, reading, discussing, experimenting or further study.
7. The material is free from distractions, conflicts or bias.
8. The production of the material is not time-consuming.

## Advantages

- These are quite cheap and economical. It develops economic value among students.
- They have great educational value. While devising such

apparatus students gain more familiarity with the underlying principles of the apparatus.

- Develops the creative and constructive instructs of the child.
- Inspires the young students and teachers to explore and invent new things.
- Develops the lower of initiative and resourcefulness in the students.
- Develops the power of scientific thinking and scientific method of problem solving.
- Inculcates the habit of diligences in the students.
- Promotes dignity of labour.
- Utilization of leisure time.
- Develops 'learning by doing' and 'leaning by living' among the students.
- Develops self-criticism, self-appraisal and self-improvement.

**Some of the Improvised Apparatus**

***Voltmeter***

Take a plastic glass and pierce two holes at its bottom. Insert two copper wires one in each hole. Fill the glass with acidulated water and invert two test tubes of water one on each wire. On connecting the wires to the two terminals of a battery, water will begin to decompose into hydrogen and oxygen which get collected in the two test tubes.

***Periscope***

Fix the mirrors in the box at an angle of $45^0$. Cut the holes on the sides of the box so that you can look into the mirrors. To demonstrate the use of periscope, shine a beam of light into one mirror in a darkened room and observe how the light beam has been beat.

***Expansion of Solids***

Take a metal rod (Iron rod/ Aluminum rod) fix it at one end and the other end of the rod is placed on a graphic plate (measuring scale plate). A burner is placed at the centre to heat the rod continuously. After some time the rod expands and we observe the variance in the measuring scale plate. With this, we conclude that solids are expanding on heating.

### *Voltmeter*

Take a small glass beaker and pour some Dil. $H_2SO_4$ and place two plates (Cu and Zn). Connect a bulb with the end of the plates with a wire. The bulb glows with this we will be able to teach the students how chemical reaction changes into Electrical Energy.

### *Diffusion of Gases*

Take a broken glass test tube (it means two sides are opened). The two ends are closed with the cotton balls dipped in $NH_3$ and Dil. HCl respectively. After few seconds a brownish ring forms it the centre of the tube. The acids of two ends are diffuse and form the ring.

In this way, we can prepare as many as improved apparatus for the concerned topic and teach the lesson effectively.

# 8

# Science Curriculum: Qualities of a Good Science Textbook

## Introduction

Curriculum is one of the most important components of Education Process. The child of today is a builder of tomorrow. It is only through a well-designed and effectively implemented curriculum that the child will be equipped to realise his inner potentials and to contribute meaningfully to nation building. Curriculum forms basis to the physical, social, aesthetic, emotional, ethical, intellectual, social, spiritual and vocational development of the child. As observed by William J. Bennett, if the teacher is the guide, the curriculum is the path. In this lesson you are going to learn about the meaning and nature of curriculum, Functions of Science Curriculum, Principles of Curriculum Construction, Defects in the Existing School Science curriculum and Qualities of a Good Science Textbook.

## Curriculum

### *Definition and Meaning of Curriculum*

The word curriculum is derived from a Latin word "currere", which means, "to run". Thus curriculum means the path or the course to be run through while a certain goal or destination is reached. It describes the ground, which pupil and teacher cover to reach the goals or objectives of education.

According to the Dictionary of Education—"Curriculum is a body of prescribed educative experiences under school supervision designed to provide an individual with the best possible training and experience to fit him for the society of which he is a part or to fit him for a trade or profession."

Alberty, A. and Alberty, E. define curriculum as, "The sum total of the student activities, which the school sponsors for the purpose of achieving its objectives."

In the words of Cunningham, "Curriculum is a tool in the hands of the artist (the teacher) to mould his materials (the pupils) according to his ideals in his studio (the school)."

According to Payne, "Curriculum consists of all the situations that the school may select and consciously organise for the purpose of developing the personality of its pupils and for making behaviour changes in them."

According to Edward, A. Crug, "Curriculum is a path to provide Learning Experiences to pupils."

From the above definitions curriculum is the soul of the process of education. It acts as a pivot in organising educational effort on some manageable basis and is undoubtedly the heart of the school and all that goes with it.

***Modern Concept of Curriculum***

The traditional concept of equating curriculum with subject knowledge is no longer justifiable. In no way, it is considered as synonym with course of study or academic subjects of instruction or syllabus. The courses of study do list much of the content and indicate many activities but they form only a part of curriculum.

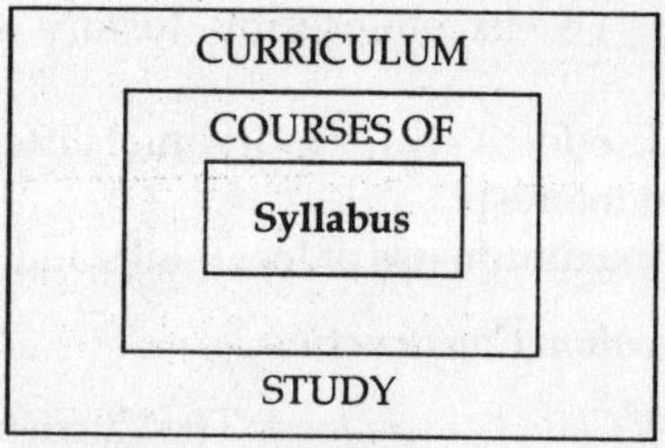


This shows that by Curriculum we mean all the educational experiences that schools provide to the pupils. The courses of studies evolve from the curriculum; syllabi are but outlines of the course content to be included in the chosen subjects.

The Secondary Education Commission (1952-53) finally expressed the broader concept of curriculum in the following terms,

"Curriculum in this context does not mean only the academic subjects traditionally taught in the schools. But it includes the totality of experiences that pupils receive through the manifold activities that go on in the school, in the classroom, library, laboratory, workshop, playgrounds, and in the numerous informal contacts between the teacher and the pupils. In this sense the whole life of the school becomes the curriculum, which can touch the life of the students in all pursuits and help evolution of balanced personality."

So it consists of contents and activities, which the school employs for the purpose of training the students. It is a total situation available to the teacher through which he makes behaviour changes. The experiences of pupils gained at school and in the community under the guidance of teachers are also included in the curriculum.

***Functions of Science Curriculum***

1. To provide pupils continuous as well as sequential experiences right from the very beginning of the school.
2. To approach science conceptually rather than factually with somewhat less emphasis on the technical applications of science.
3. To use those methods of instruction which familiarise students not only with the nature of scientific enterprise but also with the various processes of science or scientific method.
4. To provide deeper insights into the scheme of the structure of science, i.e., its philosophy, history and methods of inquiry.
5. To provide effectively for individual differences, abilities, needs and interests.
6. To make maximum use of local skills and resources.

***Principles of Curriculum Construction***

1. *Principle of Child Centeredness:* The Curriculum should be according to the interests, abilities, needs and desires of the pupils at that particular age. This principle insists on the original impulses or native propensities of the children in education.
2. *Principle of Community Centeredness:* The curriculum should determine the purpose of the society and should be prepared to fulfil the needs of the community.

3. *Principle of Integration:* There should be logical integration of the different activities and subjects to make instruction more meaningful. The curriculum should integrate the child's needs and activities.
4. *Principle of Life Centeredness:* There should be co-existence between curriculum and life. The curriculum should be related to the life of the individual in the community. It involves the preparation of the child for vocation, creation and recreation to enable him to be socially efficient, economically sufficient, intellectually alert, physically fit, professionally proficient and culturally competent.
5. *Principle of Activity Centeredness:* There should be more emphasis on learning by doing. More provision should be made for individual laboratory work and other field experiences.
6. *Principle of Creativity:* The curriculum should include those activities, which enable the child to exercise his creative and constructive powers. The objective of education is to discover and to develop special interests, tastes and aptitudes.
7. *Forward Looking Principle:* It should help the child in adjustment and prepare him for full and effective adult life. Curriculum should give due place to the future needs and requirements of the community. It should give the students a foundation of knowledge, feelings that will enable them to change according to the environment or change the environment when it is needed.
8. *Conservative Principle:* The curriculum should include all the forms of knowledge, skills and values, which the society upholds and feels to preserve and transmit through the coming generations.
9. *Principle of Elasticity and Variety:* The curriculum should not be rigid but should be changed according to the changing needs of different pupils. It should cater for the different needs, interests and abilities of the children and also to the changing conditions. It should be adapted to individual differences.
10. *Principle of Balance:* The curriculum should be framed in such a way as every aspect of life i.e., economical, social, occupational, spiritual and cultural life is given due

emphasis. It should also maintain proper balance between direct and indirect experiences, individual and social aims and among the subjects.

11. *Principle of Utility:* The curriculum should be of practical use to the pupils and hence vocational and technical education should be included in it. Due emphasis should be given to work experience.
12. *Principle of All-Round Development:* All kinds of experiences should be provided to the students so that they may develop their all powers in body, mind and spirit.
13. *Principle of Leisure:* The curriculum must prepare the child for the use of leisure time. Leisure activities such as preparation of models, participation of science club activities, collection of models and specimens should be given a prominent place in the curriculum.
14. *Principle of Correlation with Other Subjects:* Curriculum is divided into various subjects only for the sake of convenience, but now the importance of correlation is fully realised and educationists are thinking of vertical as well as horizontal correlation. So the science curriculum should be correlated with other school subjects, social and physical environment.

## Defects in the Existing Science Curriculum

The present-day school science curriculum is subject-centred and topical. It is academic in nature and deals with the theoretical generalisations.

1. It is not in conformity with the aims and objectives of teaching science.
2. It is examination ridden.
3. The concept of general science is still foreign to the curriculum.
4. It is cut off from the real life outside and is not in accordance with the needs of the pupils and the society.
5. It is not flexible but static and rigid. The same curriculum is suggested for both boys and girls, urban and rural even for various geographical conditions.
6. The depth of the subject is sacrificed at the expense of range of topics.
7. It outfits different age groups.

8. It is devoid of science activities like science clubs, exhibitions, etc.
9. There is little concern for first hand experiences.
10. There is sole emphasis on textbooks.
11. There is no place for teacher-pupil planning and largely based on opinions rather than experimentation and empirical research.

The following defects are pointed out by the Secondary Education Report in 1952-53 and have still relevance for us today.

1. The present curriculum is narrowly conceived.
2. It is bookish and theoretical.
3. It is over-crowded, without providing rich and significant contents.
4. It makes inadequate provisions for practical and other kinds of activities, which should reasonably find room in it, if it is to educate the whole of the personality.
5. It does not cater to the various needs and capacities of the adolescents.
6. It is dominated too much by examinations.
7. It does not include technical and vocational subjects, which are so necessary for training the students to take part in the industrial and economic development of the country.

About 13 years later, the Education Commission (1964-66) also confirmed the above-mentioned defects in the secondary curriculum.

**Physical Science Textbook**

*Books are keys to wisdom's treasure*

*Books are gates to lanes of pleasure*

*Books are paths that upward lead*

*Books are friends; come, let us read*

Textbooks are one of the important components in the teaching-learning process. "As is the textbook, so is the teaching-learning." It plays an important role in schools. A good variety of books for supplementary reading, periodicals and weekly newspapers are exclusively devoted to science. The science textbooks prove to be suppliers of facts and develop the appreciation and understanding of concepts and principles, their utility in daily life.

We acquire knowledge in two ways: through our direct experiences and by learning from other's experiences. A book belongs to the later type of learning source. A textbook contains material chosen according to a plan and with a specific purpose. Traditionally, a textbook has been an unavoidable instrument in any teaching-learning process. Next to the teacher's oral presentation, the textbook is considered almost synonymous with schooling. A textbook helps the teacher in teaching systematically. It will probably continue to be used both by inexperienced as well as the experienced teachers at all levels of instruction. A textbook is considered to be a course of study organised according to a set plan and a learning guide rather than a source book of information. Textbooks are usually general and comprehensive in nature. The details of any topic and relevant local examples, useful, practical problems, etc. may be lacking.

## Qualities of a Good Physical Science Textbook

It is not only the subject matter and flow of language but also the mechanical features like the paper, the printing, etc. which also play an important role in the selection of a textbook.

According to G. Mallionson the following points should be kept in mind while selecting a textbook for junior high school (secondary school) science.

The level of complexity of the textbook should be corresponding to intellectual level of the students.

- The nature of the illustrations.
- The style of writing.
- The suggestions about supplementary activities.
- The provision for individual differences.
- The clarity and organisation of material.

However, there are certain other criteria for a good science textbook.

### *(a) The Author – His Qualifications and Experience*

Only the author who has a certain amount of experience of teaching the subject should be allowed to publish a book because only he can understand the actual learning situations and difficulties of pupils. Moreover, he is conversant with the changing concepts and techniques of teaching.

Certain minimum academic qualifications may also be prescribed for the author.

***(b) Mechanical Features of the Textbook***

The quality of the paper should be fine, the printing should be appealing and the binding of the textbook should be attractive. The size of the textbook should be according to the age of the learners.

The book should contain good illustrations with sketches, diagrams, pictures, etc. The illustrations should find their proper place in the textbook so as to serve the purpose for which they stand.

***(c) The Subject Matter—Its Nature and Organisation***

The subject matter should be developed in psychological sequence. It should be according to the age, ability, interests and abilities of the students.

- Each chapter should begin with a brief introduction and end with a summary.
- The textbook should be according to the aims and objectives of science teaching.
- There should be consistency and harmony of the subject matter.
- The textbook should lead to the inculcation of scientific attitudes, disciplinary and cultural values, etc.
- The textbook should be written in lucid, simple and precise scientific language.
- A standard terminology for scientific and technical terms should be used. The English equivalents should also be given within the brackets.
- It should also contain a glossary of technical terms used in the book.
- Each chapter should contain assignments and practice exercises at the end of the chapter confirming to the following:

    *(a)* Application to life situations.
    *(b)* Suggested activities and readings.
    *(c)* New types of self-assessment tests.
    *(d)* Suggestions and experimental work of project.
    *(e)* Numerical examples where necessary.

- The textbook should contain a detailed table of contents and an index.
- The headings and sub-headings should be in bold type. The matter should be presented in varied and distinctive form.
- The textbook should be free from any type of ambiguity in language, terminology and information.
- To facilitate learning the textbook should suggest some good methods of learning.
- It is better if the textbook contains examples form the local environment and should be correlated with daily life situations and other subjects too.
- The textbook should be accompanied by a laboratory manual and a teacher's guidebook.
- The textbook should also mention the teaching aids.
- The textbook should be reasonably priced.
- It should be in accordance with the syllabus.

# 9

# Science Clubs, Fairs, Museums and Excursions

## SCIENCE CLUB

### Meaning and Importance

The present curriculum doesn't provide an opportunity for the students for self-expression, constructive activity, individual research and other projects. With this the natural urge of the students can decreasing. To chennalise the energies of students and to make proper use of talent of the students' science clubs may be organized in schools.

An organization which caters for the inculcation of scientific attitude, interest and activities, supplements the work of the class room and lab work and puts the syllabus on a practical bias may be called as science club.

Through the science club, the learning of science becomes joyful. The students learn the things without the conscious effort on their part and pursue science as a pleasant hobby. It provides an opportunity to the students for self-expression and creativity and acquaint the facts and principles of science.

### Objectives of Science Club

Some of the objectives of a science club are:

- To inculcate scientific attitude and provide opportunities for training in scientific method.
- To develop habits of exploration and creative and inventive faculties.
- To develop interest in scientific hobbies.

- To keep the students in touch with the recent advances of science and their effect on human life.
- To contact other science clubs in the neighbourhood and exchange views and information.
- To make students in particular and the public in general science minded.
- To encourage pupils to take co-operative enterprise and initiative in learning science and to develop habits of next and healthful living.

## Organization of a Science Club

Every science club should have a constitution and every member should strictly abide by it. A science club should be as:

| *Position* | *Person* | *Name of the Work* |
|---|---|---|
| Patron | Head of the Institution | Extends all types of facilities and Co-operation |
| Sponsor | The teacher -in-charge | Adviser, guide and helps in conducting of club activities. |
| Chairman | One amongst the students | Presides over the functions of the club. |
| Secretary | One amongst the students | Maintains the record of club activities and correspondence the club activities to other clubs. |
| Asst. Secretary | One amongst the students | Invites guests and also acts as secretary if in the absence of secretary. |
| Treasurer | One amongst the students | Maintain the accounts of the club. |
| Librarian | One amongst the students | Maintain the club records permanently and collect the fresh information from the other sources. |
| Store-keeper | One amongst the students | Maintain the club equipment |
| Publicity Officer | One amongst the Students | Publicises the activities of club through different means. |
| Class Representatives | One from each class | Executive committee members of the club. |

The above executive body should works for a period of one year. The body is constitutes according to electrode method. Any student can took part as a member of the club with a small membership fee.

**Activities of the Club**

Some of the science club activities are suggested as below:

- Discussions, meetings, debates, seminars etc.
- Excursions and visits to places of scientific interest.
- Science exhibitions and fairs.
- Maintenance of the class museums.
- Arranging extension lectures in science.
- Drawing charts, pictures, preparation of models etc.
- Rendering possible service to the community.
- Celebrating science days.

## SCIENCE FAIRS/EXHIBITIONS

**Meaning and Importance**

Science fairs include the exhibits as well as demonstrations. They also include talk by experts, film shows on scientific topics, debates, magic shows etc. Both the teacher and the pupils should collaborate towards the success of the fair.

The science fairs have social, intellectual, psychological and educational values. The science fair/exhibition provides an excellent opportunity for discovering and encouraging science talent.

Since 1970, NCERT organizing National Science Exhibition every year for children in New Delhi. Participants of this fair are crossed from the District, State and Regional Science Exhibition selections.

**Organization of a Science Fair**

It should be a teacher pupil activity and everything should be thought of well in advance.

**Planning**

During planning-objectives of the fair, procedure of financing, place, time and duration, facilities etc., should be considered.

**Distribution of Work**

Work should be assigned to different committees namely advisory, executive, reception, maintenance, seating, publicity etc., based on the interests and talents of the students.

**Execution**

The exhibition and other programmes like talks, demonstrations, film shows, displaying the charts, models etc.

The fair is inaugurated by a great scientists or an important person. For visit, keep it as open to all.

**Judging**

The judging should be as objective as possible by the different teams of experts.

## SCIENCE MUSEUMS

**Meaning**

'Museum' is derived from the Greek word 'mouseion' meaning 'temple of muses'. "A place of study which specializes in assembling, protecting and showing of objects, specimens and exhibits of a great variety" is called as Museum. If the place is fully equipped with all the above varieties related to science, then it is called a Science Museum.

Museums are a wonderful medium for public education. Museums are not only places of visit by pupils; they serve as sources of instructional materials to schools and students. There are thousands of museums all over the world and most of them concentrate on art, history, science and anthropology.

India starts its first ever museum in Calcutta in the year 1959 namely Birla Industrial and Technological Museum.

**Organising a School Museum**

Every school can build its own museum. The teacher in-charge has to mobilise the students to collect the natural instincts. Historical evidences, developmental theories of sciences etc. and placed them in a room. Instructions given to the students that every exhibit should be properly labelled with a brief description.

The teacher should also visit the other museum along with his students. A well-equipped museum is not only an asset to the school, but also a motivating and vitalising factor for the particular subject. Museums are permanent institutions unlike exhibitions.

**Principles of Organising a Museum**

- Every exhibit looks like an independent one, don't placed dual.
- Out of date exhibits should be replaced by suitable ones every now and then.
- Children should be given opportunities whenever possible to 'feel' the objects. A harmonious correlation of 'seeing' and 'feeling' will create confidence in the students and make learning more permanent.
- Rearrange the exhibits at suitable intervals with change in colour and place, so that they look 'new'.
- Prepare such exhibits that posses the process of public attraction.
- Additions to exhibits ought to be made for time-to-time.
- Don't overcrowd a section.

## SCIENCE EXCURSIONS

**Meaning**

'Excursion' the word usually notation mostly as a tour undertaken for recreation and pleasure. But the main aim of the excursion is impose the knowledge through direct experience. Therefore, every educational institution has given importance to it and compulsory for the study-tours, field trips, science projects etc. During such excursions pupils have concentrate learning experience in real situations.

Life in the classroom can cover only a small part of our total life and if our learning is to become full and well-rounded, we must go beyond our school walls and into the community as students and as working participants.

The field excursion was first advocated by Roussean in the Emile, first used in class teaching by Pestology in his school at verdhun in Switzerland in the first decade of 19th century.

**Educational Values or Advantages of an Excursion**

1. Through the field trips/excursions, we bring the classroom into the community and bring the problems of the community back into the classroom (School and community relation).

2. It can influence one's ideas, emotions and values (attitude change).
3. Real source materials can be studied in the field and concrete evidences obtained (community as a teaching aid).
4. Develop the responsibility, self-discipline, initiative correcting and good human relationship (moral value).
5. Excursions/field trips integrate school subjects (competition value).
6. Oral and written expressions may be stimulated (psychological value).
7. Engage the leisure time with our hobbies (disciplinary value).

## Organising an Excursion

Following are the few tips for organising an excursion:

### *Planning*

Teacher should be well in advance with the planning about the route, time schedule, transportation arrangement, finance, locations, accommodation etc. He gives assurance to the student-parents about their wards.

### *Teacher Preparation*

Before going to excursion/trip, inform the students about the important of the place; with that students get first hand information.

At the field, he helps the students if they need some clarification from him.

Use variety of learning materials to give background to do selective viewing.

### *Follow-up Activities*

- Discussions-both informal and of the panel type.
- Demonstrations about the observed things in the trip.
- Film show or photo session should be there after the trip for extend the ideas.

### *Evaluation of Excursion*

The teacher and students are evaluating their trip in the following way:

- Did the excursion serve their purpose?
- What factors accounted for its success?
- Was there sufficient time for all matters?
- Whether the route and transportation facilities are satisfactory?
- If any modifications need, they are incorporate in the other trips.

**Science in Everyday Life**

Science and Technology have changed man's life and his abilities to do work. Everything has considerably improved and it is only due to science. For leading a comfortable life we depend on science and it has showed its impact on serially changes, cultural diverse, economical, political, spiritual, transporting, medical and communication areas.. Not only the above areas, at present every operation depends on science and technology. It has also increased the rate of development of an area.

Some of the significant role played by science in your daily life:

*(i)* *Science-Agriculture:* Science has played a significant role in increasing the productivity in agriculture by developing new hybrid varieties, effective use of fertilizers, pesticides, advanced methods of cultivation, improved qualify of seeds, separation of grains from chart increased the yield of crop.

'Green revolution', white revolution' and 'Blue revolution' are some of new achievements in this field.

*(ii)* *Science and Health:* Science has contributed magnificently to this field. A number of wide varieties of medicines, vaccines and surgeries existed and have proved to be saviours of mankind.

Science is progress to give the answers to the typical diseases like AIDS, SARS, etc.

*(iii)* *Science and Industry:* Initially, the only source of energy available to man was his own muscular energy. But now machines help a lot to man in his work and at the same time saves the time.

Plastic, fiber and synthetic technology place dominant role place even from domestic needs to large and rigid articles too.

(iv) *Science and Living Conditions:* The living conditions of human beings have become sophisticated with the advent of new technologies and machines. All the gadgets in our houses are controlled by modern conditions and are user friendly, modern, comfortable, attractive and efficient.

(v) *Science and Communication*: The satellite channels have played a significant role in our lives. Now-a-days programmes of higher education to elementary education are broadcasted on Doordarshan for specific time by UGC.

With the development of computers, internet and instant communication the whole world has become a global village.

**Pollution Control and Protection of Environment**

***Pollution Control***

An undesirable change in the physical, chemical or biological characteristics of the natural of the natural environment brought about by man's activities is leads the 'pollution'.

***Pollution of Atmosphere***

Water pollution, soil pollution, sound pollution are some of the haphazard to man's life.

Government of India is also taking remedial measures to control these pollutions with the help of Pollution Control Boards' across the country.

***Environmental Protection***

Science and technology is once again striving hard to decrease this environmental pollution in the form of green house effect, global warming etc.

Day-to-day the diffusion of Ozone layer is increasing due to environmental pollution. If we can't protect it, the infrared rays from the sun directly attack the human beings and make many haphazard.

Consuming of the articles with chloroform carbons can be reduced.

The new technology also stepping forward in protection of the environment.

## Role of Voluntary Science Organizations in Popularising Science

### *Non-Formal Science Teaching*

The National Policy on Education (NPE, 1986) has laid considerable emphasis on strengthening the science education in the school education system. The NPE, 1986 envisages extension through every effort of science education not only to those who are in the formal school system but also to those who have remained outside the system under non-formal and adult education programmes.

The non-formal mode of education differs from the formal one in that it is an organized activity with educational purposes carried on outside the highly structured framework of formal educational system to keep in line with the levels of academic standards.

The Government of India has given high priority to this mode of education through five year planes, progrmmes like Balwadis, Non-Formal Centres of Education, Nehru Yuvak Kendras and provides education with the help of UNICEF and UNESCO for the group of 6-15 through non-formal methodology.

At present not only the Government of India is provide this type of education, many science organizations access the country are popularizing science education through their non-formal science teaching modes.

### *Voluntary Organisations in Popularising Science*

There are many voluntary science organisations at various parts of the country. Working towards popularising science among masses and universalization of science education. Some are discussed here.

1. *Jawahar Bala Bhavans (JBBs):*

- Established in 1966.
- Spread over in 12 states headquarters.
- Cater the needs of children's upto the age of 14 years.
- Activities like dancing, painting, clay work, carpentary, drama, debates, star-gazing, stamp collections, radio repairs, gardening etc.
- Conducting training programmes to the teachers.
- Publish different scientific magazines, training handbooks etc.

2. *Vikram Sarabhai Community Science Centre: (VSCSC)*

- Established in 1966 by Vikram Sarabhai.
- Located at Ahamadabad, Gujarat State.
- Founding Agency – Nehru Foundation.
- Promote social and educational development through the science and technology.
- Activities like science film shows, science exhibitions, popular science lectures, science hobbies, science puppet-shows, open-house programmes etc.
- Brought out some magazines, science newspaper, audio-visual aids.
- Training facilities to students and teachers.

3. *Kishore Bharathi (KB)*

- Established in 1971 by Kishore Bharathi.
- Located at Palia Piparia (Village), Hoshangabad (Dt), Madhya Pradesh State.
- Improving science education methods and techniques based on the needs of rural community.
- In collaboration with the State Government, organizing curriculum, learning methods, examination systems and training to teachers especially for cater the needs of rural school students throughout the state.
- Conducting Science Exhibitions in the villages.

4. *Ekalavya Science Teaching Project (ESTP)*

- Established in 1972 by Kishore Bharathi as pilot project of 16 rural high schools.
- Start at Rasulia (village), Housangabad (Dt), M.P. State with the help of friends rural centre and State Education Department.
- Spread over 206 rural high schools in 1978.
- Priority given to product, process and discovery approaches in the curriculum.
- Insert the simple concepts which are familiar by the rural students in the syllabus and remove the modern scientific concepts like chemical symbol, atomic structure, etc.
- Forming the students into 'Tele's' (means a group of four students) and provide them science experiments, discussions, excursions for brush up their mind themselves.

- Priority given to Environmental Education and Heuristic Method.
- Evaluation made especially on scientific skills, attitudes and understanding of the concepts.

5. *Visveswarayya Industrial and Technological Museum (VITM)*

- Established in 1965.
- Located at Bangalore.
- Conducting regional science exhibitions to develop the divergent thinking among students and teachers.
- Providing training facilities to the teachers in teaching modules, experiments, workshop tools of South Indian Sates.
- Conducting individual/ grouped project works, seminars, quiz programmes, lecture-cum-demonstration techniques to the students in collaboration with National Council of Science Museum (NCSM), New Delhi.
- Publishing various teachers hand books, Training Modules, instructional material, different improvised apparatus and its details etc.

6. *Kerala Shastra Sahitya Parisha (KSSP)*

- Established in 1963.
- Spread over throughout Kerala State with 600 units.
- Around 10,000 members comprising with all professionalisms and public.
- Conducting science campaigns, science centres.
- Developing scientific tools like smokeless stove, high power stove.
- Conducting rural science forms, medical camps, health and environmental campaigns at villages and in rural schools.
- Conducting talent tests to the elementary, high school and college students.
- Participated in a total literacy campaign, excise prohibition campaigns.

7. *Andhra Pradesh Science Centre (APSC)*

- Established in 1974.
- Located at Hyderabad.
- Conducting training programmes to teachers in teaching-learning material, topical and concentric methods of

curriculum approaches and innovative techniques of science teaching.

- Conducting science exhibitions at district and state level, science seminars, quiz programmes etc.
- Transmit the science and technology cater the needs to rural areas through District Science Centres (DSC).

8. *Jana Vignana Vedika (JVV)*

- Established on 28-2-1988 (on national science day).
- Located at Vijayawada, A.P. State.
- Founded by Department of Science and Technology (DST), and National Council of Science and Technology Communications (NCSTC).
- Around 1 lakh members with all professionalisms and public.
- Collecting annual membership fee Rs. 10, and Rs. 5 for employees and unemployees (students) respectively to supportive to the organization activities.
- It has Organising Committees from village to state level.
- Activities like Medical and Health campaigns, science Magic workshops, total literacy campaign, Environmental awareness among the public.
- Training facilities to students and teachers in science. Concepts and in improvised apparatus (low cost).
- Conducting National days in school premises promoting National Integration.
- Publish several scientific pomplets, science magazines, etc.

9. *Konaseema Science Parishad (KSP)*

- Established in 1984 by C.V. S. Sarma ( National best teacher awardee).
- Started at Amalapuram, East Godavari (Dt), A.P. State.
- Developing Scientific Knowledge among school pupils and common men.
- Suggested the remedial measures and solutions to the day-to-day problems in the form of formal and non-formal mode especially in science.
- Conducting science meeting, seminars, and campaigns in the village level to state level.
- Published nearly 37 popular science textbooks, 2000 science essays, 150 children science stories.

# 10

# Evaluation in Science

## Evaluation – Concept

Evaluation is a recent scientific concept and more comprehensive them more measurement. It is a continuous appraisal of the achievement of the aims of education as well as the methods of teaching and learning with a view to continuous improvement that educations become dynamic and self-developing. Evaluation exercises a great influence on the pupils study habits and teachers methods of instruction and thus help not only to measure educational achievement.

According to Bradfield J.M. "Evaluation is the assignments of symbols to phenomenon, in order to characterize the worth or value of a phenomenon usually with reference to some social, cultural or scientific standards."

## Measurement and Evaluation

Measurement I concerned primarily with the grade placement of an individual; evaluation is primarily concerned with its use to improve teaching and learning. The main differences between the two are.

| *Measurement* | *Evaluation* |
|---|---|
| 1. It gives only quantity | 1. Its gives quantity and quality two |
| 2. Its scope is limited | 2. Its scope is widen |
| 3. It helps in determine the present status | 3. It helps the evaluation to make an estimate of his future progress |

*(Contd.)*

| *Measurement* | *Evaluation* |
|---|---|
| 4. It doesn't continue process | 4. It is a life long process. |
| 5. It is a part of evaluation | 5. Without measurement evaluation doesn't consideration. |
| 6. It doesn't gives the totality of a child | 6. It teachers every aspect of the students education. |

**Process of the Evaluation**

In the previous steps, we come across that educational evaluation is a broad concept which involves the instructional objectives, content/ subject matter, learning experiences and evaluation procedures. These all are inter connected to one another.

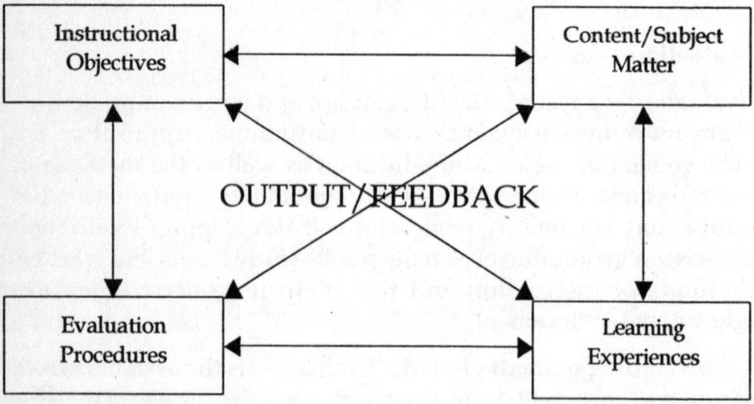


The above evaluation process cycle clearly gives that a teacher must followed the steps :

1. First and foremost its to formulating and selecting worth while objectives of teaching in a subject.
2. The objectives and the behavioural changes are brought through proper content and subject matter.
3. Learning experiences can be brought through reading good number of textbooks listening and acquiring the subject matter.
4. In accordance learning experience, use devise proper evaluation procedures.
5. The expected output can be obtained and suggest in turns by results or behavioural changes (i.e., feedback).

## Types of Evaluation

Evaluation can be classified into four types:

(i) *Formative Evaluation:* It concerned with making decisions relating to forming or development of students as well as of the courses. It is monitor the instructional process to determine whether learning is takes place as planned. The major function of formative evaluation in the classroom is to provide feedback to the teacher and to the student about how things are going. It requires the gathering of fairly detailed information on frequent occasions.

(ii) *Summative Evaluation:* It is conducted at the end of an instructional segment to determine if learning is sufficiently completed to warrant moving the learn to the next segment of instruction. In other words, it is concerned with making judgments about a finished product or process.

**Table-1**

**Characteristics that Distinguish Classroom Formative and Summative Evaluation**

| *Characteristics* | *Formative* | *Summative* |
|---|---|---|
| 1. Purpose | Monitor Progress | Check final status |
| 2. Content focus | Detailed, narrow scope | General, broad scope |
| 3. Methods | Observation, daily tests | Tests or final examinations, projects |
| 4. Frequency | Daily | Weakly or fortnight |

The terms formative and summative were introduced by Scriven (1967).

(iii) *Diagnostic Evaluation:* It helps in identifying the defects or specific weakness or problems, of the learner during the course or in the beginning or the teaching-learning process. Sometimes it used in designing the courses or curricular to fulfill the needs of the learner.

## Tools of Evaluation

A tool of evaluation is used in education as a technique that will facilitate the process of measuring and recording the characteristics of pupils. The following are the some of main tools of Evaluation in education:

(i) Tests
(ii) Questionnaires
(iii) Check Lists
(iv) Rating Scales
(v) Observation
(vi) Anecdotal Record
(vii) Interview.

### Test

A test is defined to estimate that the acquire knowledge or situation by the person after a certain period of instruction. Examinations and tests have been regarded as the major tools of evaluation in education.

Achievement tests constitute an important tool in school evaluation programme. According to N.M. Dowinie "any list that measures the attainments or accomplishments of an individual after a period of training or learning in called an Achievement Test."

*Objective Type Tests*

"An objective type test is importing to the objectivity rather than the subjectivity." It tests the factual information. There are several types of objective tests used in Evaluation. Few of them are given in the following diagram:

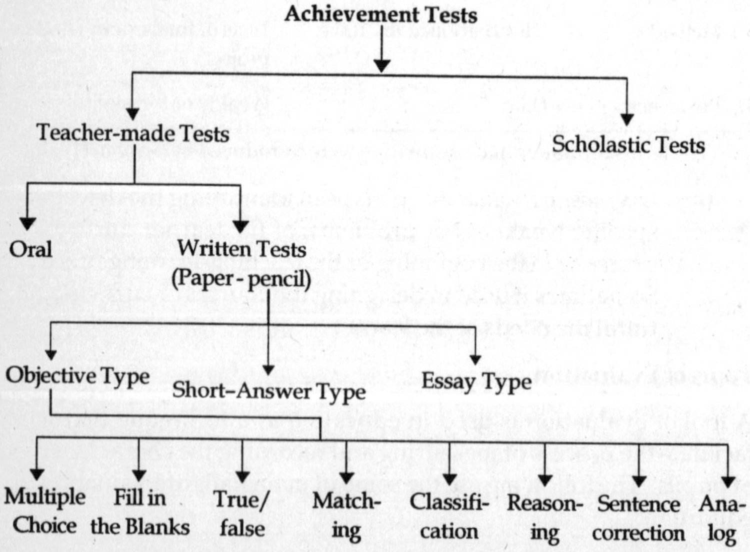

*Advantages*

1. Extensive sampling.
2. Objectivity of scoring.
3. Economy of time.
4. No bluffing.
5. Equalicy of time opportunity.
6. Speed and accuracy.
7. Testing all the objectives.
8. Easy to conducts and scoring.

*Limitations*

1. Often Antiguans.
2. Constructions of these tests are difficulty and considerable cost.
3. Lack of availability of skilled persons in construction.
4. Providing guesting priority.
5. Fail to measure the intellectual skills of students.

*Short-Answer Type Tests:* These types of tests are testing high through -providing. They used in testing somewhat we actually expert from the students. They test the objectivity as well as subjectivity of the student. Because the student answer to these type of questions in the forms of a few sentences or words.

*Essay Type Tests:* The essay type test is allow the student in relative freedom of response in answering the question, at the same time-to-time requires the student to recall rather than recognisition information and sequentially express his views clearly and concisely. It prior to high subjectivity.

*Advantages*

1. Easy to construct.
2. Developing good study habits and also reading and writing skill.
3. Controlling the mass copying and guessing.
4. Free to express his in heart ability skill, ideas.
5. More priority given to application and skill objectives.
6. Developing logical reasoning, simplifying and explaining.
7. Promoting the language caliber and matter organization.

*Limitations*

1. Low validity and reliability.
2. Less objectivity and high subjectivity.
3. They not test the real knowledge.
4. Lack of comprehensiveness.
5. Encouraging rote memory or by hate.
6. Time taken in scoring.
7. Can't test all the objectives.
8. Can't caver all the teaching-learning points (syllabus).

## *Questionnaire*

Questionnaire is a set of questions for securing answers (information seeking) from a sample of population.

The information collected with a questionnaire helps in evaluation of personality traits, interests, attitudes, applauds etc., sometimes it helps in providing guidance and councelling.

## *Check Lists*

It is a simple tool or evaluation which tests various aspects of an individual's behavioural adjustment. Sometimes it useful to evaluate the physical conditions of the people's institutions or objects.

## *Rating Scales*

It is a device by which the opinion concerning a trait can be systematized. Rating is a term to express an opinion or judgement. They are usually expressed on a scale of value is also called rating scales.

For Example: How beautiful she is?

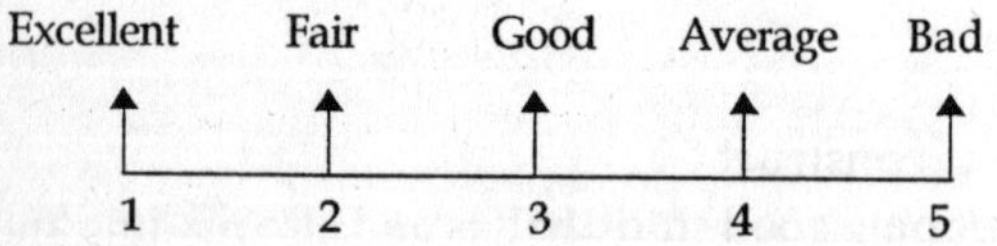


**Types**

1. *Numerical* — 3-point numerical scale; 5-point numerical scale; 3-point numerical scale — In which numbers are assigned to each trait. The above example is 5-point rating scale.

2. *Graphic* : To rate a person on a particular trait in descriptive phases at various points.

*Ex :* He attends the meeting.

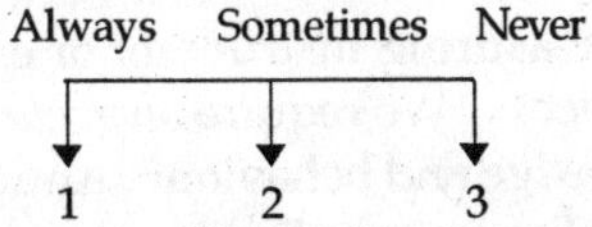


3. *Method of Paired Comparison:* The rater compares each person being rated with respect to the trait of every other individual interms of 'equal', 'better' or 'worse'.
4. *Man of Man Scale:* An individual is asked to rate the person to be rated by comparing him to a person already rated and assigned a position on the scale. The rate is assigned his position.
5. *Score Cards:* In which whatever is being rated is analysed into its component parts.

### *Observation*

Observation is a tool to evaluate an external behaviour of persons in controlled uncontrolled situation can be verified and recorded. They are two types:

1. Direct observation – controlled and natural direct observation.
2. Indirect observation – controlled and natural indirect observation.

### *Anecdotal Record*

It is a record of written description of a specific incident/ s, which a teacher has observed the students behaviour from time-to-time.

Previously, it is supplied to every student after completion of his S.S.L.C./S.S.C. But in the year 1985, the A.P. State Government is winding the record in school system.

### *Interview*

It is the face-to-face method of collecting information. It is used in guiding the student, diagnosing and counselling purpose too.

They are two types:

1. Structured interview seeking the information for a list of prepared items.
2. Unstructured interview-seeking information spontaneous items but not previously prepared.

**Qualities of a Good Test**

The selection of a measuring instrument or examination or test is not a haphazard process. We require an accurate tool to assess the students' real knowledge and behaviour. An accurate test or a good test must need the following qualities:

**1. *Validity***

It refers to the test quality to measure what it is intended to measure. According to "A test is valid, when it measures truly and accurately the ability or quality one wants to appraise." It also referred as truthfulness' of the test.

*Factors Affecting the Validity of a Test*

(a) *Cultural Influences:* Cultural background of a person including socio economic status influence the general factor of the intelligence of a person.
(b) *Response Sets:* Too many of these are most likely to reduce the logical and empirical validities of a test.
(c) *Lack of Clarity in Direction:* Lack of proper instructions, language clarity usage of meaningful words are use in the test lead decrease the validity.
(d) *Excess Reliability:* A test having large number of items it that leads to low validity.

*Types*

(i) *Content Validity:* A test is adequately comes both the content and objectives of the subject matter on which the test is based.
(ii) *Face Validity:* It doesn't refer to what the test actually measures but refers to what the test seems to measure.
(iii) *Construct Validity:* It refers to the extent to which the test measures a particular characteristic of an individual i.e., individuals' actual achievement of instructional objectives.
(iv) *Concurrent Validity:* This type can distinguish between two or more groups of individuals whose status at the time of testing is different.

**2. *Reliability***

It refers a test is reliable if it measures efficiently what it purposes to measure or what it does measure. A test is reliable i.e., it gives same rating to the student even if he is examined by different examiners or even different times by the same examiner. Simply it refers as "consistency" of a test.

*Factors Affecting Reliability*

(a) *The Length of the Test:* The longer test is more reliable than a shorter one i.e. a considerable number of questions need a test.
(b) *Objectivity in Scoring:* Priority given to objective based questions.
(c) *Clarity of Instructions:* The instructions should not ambiguous.

*Methods of Determination*

(a) *Test – Retest (Co-Efficient of Stability):* Pre test and post test are done on a same test item. The results of correlation give high for post test gives the reliability of the test.
(b) *Split – Half Method (Co-Efficient of Equivalence):* Either dividing the test items equally or odd and even then correlation of the two halves. From this we can get reliability by applying spearman – Brown formula $r$: $\dfrac{2r\frac{1}{2}}{1+r\frac{1}{2}}$

r1 = reliability coefficient of whole test

r 1/2 = reliability of half of test.

(c) *Parallel form (Co-Efficient of Stability and Equivalence):* The parallel form of test items i.e., in the form of content and difficulty are prepared and found the correlation between them.
(d) *K-R. Method (Co-Efficient of Internal Consistency):* Items in a test has common with another.

**3. *Objectivity***

"The degree to which equally complement users get the same result." It eliminates the examiner's personal opinion; bias or judgment on the given test.

### 4. *Practicability*

Easy to administration, scoring and low cost in preparation. It should be according to abilities of the sample.

## Scholastic Achievement Test

### *Meaning*

Achievement tests are to measure the extent learning of the students. These are diagnosing the students learning strengths and weakness. The achievement test is predominate procedure at present to assessing the progress of the pupils. These are prepared by the classroom teachers to test the students' progress and test of his instruction. "A test which is constructed based on the objectives formed and tested is called scholastic achievement test."

### *Construction of Weightage Tables*

Every teacher can construct a scholastic achievement test based on these points.

1. The content, time allocation and maximum marks;
2. Framing the objectives and test items; and
3. Allot the sufficient score to the item according to the level of difficulty. All these are depends on the following tables:

*(a) Weightage to Objectives*

Weightage must be properly cover to each objective.

| *Sl.No.* | *Objective* | *Marks Allotted* | *Percentage* |
|---|---|---|---|
| 1. | Knowledge | 8 | 32 |
| 2. | Understanding | 6 | 24 |
| 3. | Application | 6 | 24 |
| 4. | Skill | 5 | 20 |
| | Total | 25 | 100 |

*(b) Weightage to Content*

Distribute equally the content and properly coverage weightage to sub-content.

| Sl.No. | Sub-Units | Marks Allotted | Percentage |
|---|---|---|---|
| 1. | Measuring Mass | 10 | 40 |
| 2. | Time Measurement | 9 | 36 |
| 3. | Simple-pendulum-introduction, formulas | 6 | 24 |
| | Total | 25 | 100 |

*(c) Weightage to Test Items*

Weightage to be given properly to the each type of test items.

| Sl.No. | Test Item | No. of Questions | Marks Allotted | Percentage |
|---|---|---|---|---|
| 1. | Objective based | 10 | 10 | 40 |
| 2. | Short answered based | 5 | 10 | 40 |
| 3. | Essay based | 1 | 5 | 20 |
| | Total | 16 | 25 | 100 |

*(d) Weightage to Difficulty Level*

To discriminate the students, the test fulfill the needs of their difficulty level:

| S.No | Difficulty Level | Marks Allotted | Percentage |
|---|---|---|---|
| 1. | Easy level | 7 | 28 |
| 2. | Average level | 11 | 44 |
| 3. | Difficulty level | 7 | 28 |
| | Total | 25 | 100 |

***Preparation of Blue-Print***

It is a three dimensional tables consists of contents, objectives and test items. It occupies a prominent place in constructing the scholastic achievement test. With this table, we can easy to understand a question in the test can question based on which objective, in which content it takes and the type of question.

***Preparation of a Question Paper***

On the lines of weightage tables and Blue Print the question paper should be prepared. No question can be repeat and take care on

| *Objectives* | *Knowledge* | | | *Understand* | | | *Application* | | | *Skill* | | | *Total* |
|---|---|---|---|---|---|---|---|---|---|---|---|---|---|
| *Sub-Units* | O | S.A | E | O | S.A | E | O | S.A | E | O | S.A | E | |
| Measuring Mass | $(1)^{1}$ | $(1)^{2}$ | – | $(1)^{1}$ | – | – | $(1)^{1}$ | – | – | – | – | $(1)^{5}$ | $(5)^{10}$ |
| Time measurement | $(1)^{1}$ | $(1)^{2}$ | – | $(1)^{1}$ | $(1)^{2}$ | – | $(1)^{1}$ | $(1)^{2}$ | – | – | – | – | $(6)^{9}$ |
| Simple Pendulum | $(2)^{2}$ | – | – | $(2)^{2}$ | – | – | – | $(1)^{2}$ | – | – | – | – | $(5)^{6}$ |
| Sub-Total | $(4)^{4}$ | $(2)^{4}$ | – | $(4)^{4}$ | $(1)^{2}$ | – | $(2)^{2}$ | $(2)^{4}$ | – | – | – | $(1)^{5}$ | $(16)^{25}$ |
| Total | | $(6)^{8}$ | | | $(5)^{6}$ | | | $(4)^{6}$ | | | $(1)^{5}$ | | |

*Note:* Numerals within the brackets are question numbers.
Numerals outside the brackets are allotment of marks.

leading questions. Instructions should be clearly given. Preliminaries namely class, subject, maximum time and marks and the Contents of the test should be neatly typed boldly on the question paper.

Question paper should be divided into three sections with objective type, short-answer type and essay type questions. Section–A contains 10 objective based questions (3 questions for multiple choice and fill in the blanks respectively with 1 mark for each question; 2 questions for True/False and Matching type questions respectively with 1 mark for each question). Section–B have 5 short answered questions with 2 marks for each question and Section-C has to be awarded with 5 marks of 1 Essay type question.

Take care in typographical error and visibility.

### *Scoring Key*

While preparing a question paper besides the examiner prepares a scoring key. It helps if other than the paper setter in evaluation awarding the marks for the respected question. It gives the test is as a culture free test. A model of the scoring key is as on page no. 187.

### *Question/Item-wise Analysis*

After completion of the question paper and scoring key, the paper setter should analysis the each and every question that it satisfies the expected objectives contents, and difficulty level of the students or not. A model of the question-wise analysis is given under:

| *Sl.No.* | *Expected Answer* | *Marks for Each Item* | *Total Marks* |
|---|---|---|---|
| 1. | | | |
| 2. | | | |
| 3. | | | |
| 4. | | | |
| 5. | | | |
| 6. | | | |
| 7. | | | |
| 8. | | | |
| 9. | | | |
| 10. | | | |
| 11. | | | |
| 12. | | | |
| 13. | | | |
| 14. | | | |
| 15. | | | |
| 16. | | | |

| *Question Number* | *Objective* | *Analysis* | *Sub-Unit* | *Type of Question* | *Marks Awarded* | *Allotted Time* | *Level of Difficulty* |
|---|---|---|---|---|---|---|---|
| 1. | | | | | | | |
| 2. | | | | | | | |
| 3. | | | | | | | |
| 4. | | | | | | | |
| 5. | | | | | | | |
| 6. | | | | | | | |
| 7. | | | | | | | |
| 8. | | | | | | | |

*(Contd.)*

| Question Number | Objective | Analysis | Sub-Unit | Type of question | Marks Awarded | Allotted Time | Level of Difficulty |
|---|---|---|---|---|---|---|---|
| 9. | | | | | | | |
| 10. | | | | | | | |
| 11. | | | | | | | |
| 12. | | | | | | | |
| 13. | | | | | | | |
| 14. | | | | | | | |
| 15. | | | | | | | |
| 16. | | | | | | | |

### *Individual Marking Scheme*

After conducting the test, the teacher should prepare the individual scoring scheme. It helps the teacher to know the individual interest on the contents and type of item. A model of the individual scoring scheme is given under.

### *Analysis and Interpretation of Scores*

The obtained scores of the individuals (Raw scores) are tested with the statistical techniques namely measures of central tendency (Mean, Median and Mode), Measurer of dispersion (Range, Quartile Deviation, Mean Deviation, Standard Deviation and Variance), Measures of divergence (Skewness and Kurtosis). With all these we can estimate the students' innate knowledge on the subject.

The scores are plotted into different graphs namely Histograms, Frequently Polygons, Upper/Lower Cumulative Frequency curves and Ozive curve. With these, a person can get glance of idea about the standard of the students, class and teaching of the teacher.

For knowledge the difficulty level of the items, item difficulty index, item discrimination index are also calculated.

After all interpretation of the above statistical analysis the teacher inform the students about their level of knowledge, the area in which they lag behind, the type of questions which they felt difficulty. The teacher should explain the proper remedial measure to the students for their up liftment.

| *Sl. No.* | *Name of the Student* | *Item Number and Marks Awarded* | | | | | | | | | | | | | | | | | *Total Marks* |
|---|---|---|---|---|---|---|---|---|---|---|---|---|---|---|---|---|---|---|---|
| | | Q. No | 1 | 2 | 3 | 4 | 5 | 6 | 7 | 8 | 9 | 10 | 11 | 12 | 13 | 14 | 15 | 16 | (25) |
| | | Max. Marks | (1) | (1) | (1) | (1) | (1) | (1) | (1) | (1) | (1) | (1) | (2) | (2) | (2) | (2) | (2) | (5) | |
| 1. | | | | | | | | | | | | | | | | | | | |
| 2. | | | | | | | | | | | | | | | | | | | |
| 3. | | | | | | | | | | | | | | | | | | | |
| 4. | | | | | | | | | | | | | | | | | | | |
| 5. | | | | | | | | | | | | | | | | | | | |
| 6. | | | | | | | | | | | | | | | | | | | |
| 7. | | | | | | | | | | | | | | | | | | | |
| 8. | | | | | | | | | | | | | | | | | | | |
| 9. | | | | | | | | | | | | | | | | | | | |
| 10. | | | | | | | | | | | | | | | | | | | |
| 11. | | | | | | | | | | | | | | | | | | | |
| 12. | | | | | | | | | | | | | | | | | | | |
| 13. | | | | | | | | | | | | | | | | | | | |
| 14. | | | | | | | | | | | | | | | | | | | |
| 15. | | | | | | | | | | | | | | | | | | | |
| 16. | | | | | | | | | | | | | | | | | | | |

# 11

# Concepts of Teaching and Levels of Teaching

## Introduction

Teaching is a social process on which the political system, social philosophy, values and culture of every nation leave their impression. The political system and philosophical ideology of a nation will have an impact on the teaching process of the country. H.C. Morrison has defined teaching in an autocratic country as an intimate contact between a more, mature personality and a less mature one which is designed to further the education of the latter i.e., the teacher impresses the students according to his own will. In contrast, in a democracy N.L. Gage defines teaching as inter-personal influence aimed at changing the behaviour potential of another person i.e., not only the teacher influences the student but also the reverse also happens. Thus, we can conclude that teaching is a bipolar process. Its one pole is the teacher and the other is the student. In this process of mutual interaction the efforts of the teacher are called teaching and the task performed by the learner is called learning.

Teaching is a highly skilled job and therefore requires adequate training. Every teacher must have a clear understanding of his task – its meaning and intricacies involved. In this unit we shall be defining the term teaching and understand the mechanism of teaching through its various dimensions of teaching-variables, operations, phases and levels.

## CONCEPTS OF TEACHING

Historical development of the term teaching reveals that prior to the 20th century, teaching was thought of as more or less a skilled trade, in which one went with a complete command of knowledge armed with skill of explanation and testing. From the 1920's and 1930's, there was a growing tendency for education to be thought as a science because it was hypothesised that teaching is an organised effort to draw the best out of a child.

B.O. Smith defines teaching as a system of actions involving an agent, an end in view, and a situation including two sets of factors those over which the agent has no control (class size, size of classroom, physical characteristics of student's etc.) and those that he can modify (ways of asking questions about instruction and structuring of information or ideas gained. Thus Smith considers teaching to be a tri-polar purpose involving.

*An agent – the source, human or material that tries to produce learning*
*A goal or target that is to be achieved through the process of teaching and*
*The intervening variable consisting of learning or teaching situation or environment. (Human or material conditions and instructional methods)*

Admiral Amidon defines teaching as inter-active process, primarily classroom talk which takes place between teacher and student and occurs during certain definable activities.

Clark in his definition tried to broaden the very scope of teaching by terming it as a set of all those organised activities that might result in bringing some change in the behaviour of the student or learner.

Green in his definition tried to delimit the boundary and scope of teaching by terming it as a profession or occupation in which the task of the teacher is to perform for the development of the child.

- Teaching is a complex social phenomenon.
- Teaching is influenced by social and human factors. But human and social factors are dynamic – continuously changing and evolving and so is teaching.

**A. Teaching is an Art**

According to Douglas teacher acts as a director of learning activities in the classroom and also he calls upon his store of available scientific knowledge and upon his knowledge of young people and how they learn, the teacher really performs much as an artist who uses whatever materials and procedures may seem to contribute best to realizing the goals or images he has in mind. Thus teaching is considered to be an art because it involves skills to disseminate knowledge, to maintain the interest and attention of the learner and the delicate handling of the problems of the learner to modify his behaviour.

**B. Teaching is a Science**

Teaching involves a repertoire of techniques, procedures and skills that can be systematically studied, described and improved. Davis advocates a scientific approach to teaching and says that teaching is a process of managing human behaviour for learning.

UNESCO's "Learning to be" document has described teaching as a science and says that as in all sciences, our time has witnessed sweeping changes in pedagogy, to the point where the concept itself has changed. A body of related disciplines has led to reinforcement of the scientific aspects of pedagogy. It also says that what once was as art—the art of teaching—is now a science built on firm foundations and linked to psychology, anthropology, philosophy, cybernetics, linguistics and many other disciplines.

Thus teaching can be considered to be an applied science because it incorporates systematic and methodical approach. The system and method, the experimentation and trial, the probing and enquiry which are the bases of any scientific knowledge are the basis of teaching also, hence it is definitely a science.

Teaching is thus not only a science but an amalgamation of philosophy and sprinkling of art.

**C. Teaching is a Profession**

Teaching as profession places varied demands on its practitioners–teachers like exceptional qualities, skills and sincere devotion to human progress. Teaching stresses the involvement of intellectual competence, the ability to perform the required skills in order to liberate humanity from ignorance. The advancements in the field of education have given a stature and dignity to the profession.

**D. Teaching is Basically a Communication Process**

It involves a system of actions, which are varied in form and are related to content and student behaviour commensurate with the existing physical and social conditions. Teaching is what a teacher does with his students for causing the latter to learn something.

**E. Teaching is Amenable to Scientific Observation and Analysis**

What is going on during the teaching process can be observed, analysed and assessed through teacher behaviour, teacher - student interaction and the change in behaviour of the students?

**F. Teaching can Take Place through Various Forms**

The various forms of teaching are: formal and informal; formational or informational; directional or instructional; training, conditioning or indoctrination; telling, showing or doing; descriptive or remedial etc.

**Characteristics of Effective Teachers/Teaching**

Teaching broadly means 'Causing to Learn'. I think you would agree that nothing has been taught until it has been learned and effective teaching is possible only if it leads to effective learning.

The following are the main characteristics of effective teaching

***(i) Effective Teaching is Stimulating***

Aim of teaching is not merely to impart knowledge or information; it is to arouse the will to learn in the children. Effective teaching inspires learners and stimulates students to be active participants in the teaching-learning process.

***(ii) Effective Teaching is Well-Planned***

Teaching is not a one shot, one time affair. It can extend over a period of few days to few months to complete a topic/unit.

To accomplish this stage-wise activity the teaching act has to be planned systematically. The planning should make provisions for modification in case of emergencies.

***(iii) Effective Teaching is Democratic***

We are living in a democracy and education should prepare the students for leading their future life. Hence, the atmosphere in the class should be democratic. Methods of teaching and content should be selected in such a way that it involves active participation of students.

### *(iv) Effective Teaching is Kind and Sympathetic*

A successful teaching requires the teacher to be kind and sympathetic and he should be able to sort-out the difficulties and doubts of the students in subject matter and other instances also.

### *(v) Effective Teaching in Diagnostic, Remedial and Connective*

Today, we have at our disposal tools that help us diagnose the weaknesses, capabilities and intelligence of students. The teacher after assessing the students can provide remedial measures to overcome the disabilities or backwardness. Effective teaching can also help in modifying and correcting lapses and lacunae identified.

### *(vi) Effective Teaching Requires Competent Teachers*

The following are some characteristics, which are indispensable for effective teachers.

- Teacher is intelligent.
- Teachers is confident and in complete command with the content.
- Teacher can communicate effectively.
- Teacher is aware of psychological bases of learning and is able to modify student behaviour, motivate them and assess individual differences.
- Teacher is an effective planner and executor. He is able to formulate objectives and use varied methods.
- Teacher is an effective personality.
- Effective teaching requires teachers with specific traits.

Charter and Wales have identified twenty-five traits of an effective teacher. They are:

1. Adaptability
2. Attractiveness
3. Breadth of interest (interest in community, profession, students)
4. Carefulness (accuracy, definiteness, thoroughness)
5. Considerateness (appreciativeness, courtesy, tact, sympathy, kindness)

6. Co-operation (helpfulness, loyalty)
7. Dependability (consistency)
8. Enthusiasm (alertness, animation, inspiration)
9. Fluency
10. Forcefulness (courage, decisiveness, firmness, purposefulness)
11. Good judgement (discretion, foresight, insight, intelligence)
12. Health
13. Honesty
14. Industry (patience, perseverance)
15. Leadership (initiative, self-confidence)
16. Magnetism (approachability, cheerfulness, optimism, sense of humour, sociability, pleasing voice)
17. Neatness
18. Open-mindedness
19. Originality (imaginative, resourcefulness)
20. Progressiveness (ambition)
21. Promptness (dispatch, punctuality)
22. Refinement (conventionality, good taste, modesty, morality, simplicity)
23. Scholarship (intellectual curiosity)
24. Self-control (calmness, dignity, poise, reserve)
25. Thrift.

**Objectives of Teaching**

Teaching is a purposeful, dynamic and continuous process. The following are some of the broad objectives of teaching. They are as follows:

- To impart knowledge.
- To provide skill training.
- To bring about attitudinal and behavioural changes.
- To help students to adjust in a better way.
- To make the student a best learner and best thinker.
- To enable students to be good taskmasters and decision-makers.

**Variables of Teaching**

***Meaning of Variable***

A variable is defined as 'Any response or behaviour, which can take different degrees.' Teaching is a multi-faceted interaction process.

A teacher cannot teach in vacuum. A student's presence is essential for carrying out the task of teaching and the objectives of teaching can only be accomplished with the help of suitable teaching-learning material, methods and devices, and teaching-learning environment etc. Thus, teaching can be considered to be an interactive process involving the interaction of a number of variables.

Considering teaching as an interactive process, the variables responsible for such an interaction are classified as:

*(i)* Independent variable.
*(ii)* Dependent variable.
*(iii)* Intervening variable.

*(i)* *Independent Variable:* An independent variable is that variable in which the experimenter cannot bring about a change but uses it to bring about a change in the dependent variable. In the teaching-learning process, the teacher is independent variable. He is free to act in the process. He plans, organises, leads and controls the process of teaching so that desirable outcomes may be obtained. He has to handle his teaching activities and all the intervening variables in such a way that the desired behavioural changes can be brought out leading to the fulfillment of the planned objectives.

*(ii)* *Dependent Variable: Learner/Student:* The dependent variable is that variable which acquires changes as a result of changes occurred in some other dependent variable or due to the efforts of the independent variable. In the process of teaching, it is the student who is subjected to changes and development through the efforts of change. The student is dependent on the teacher for seeking behavioural changes and development.

*(iii)* *Intervening Variable:* Techniques, methods and content. Intervening variable is one that is active in between an independent and dependent variable which interferes / aids the process.

In the case of teaching-learning process contents, methods and techniques of teaching, tactics and strategies, management of instructional material and teaching environment etc., are all known as intervening variables. They are responsible for bringing about a desirable interaction between the teachers and the taught by producing proper teaching environment, teaching material and facilities and creating appropriate learning conditions or situations.

***Functions of Teaching Variable***

In the teaching–learning process the variables perform the following functions:

1. Diagnostic functions,
2. Prescriptive functions, and
3. Evaluative functions.

1. *Diagnostic Functions:* In the task of bringing about desirable changes in the behaviour of students the teacher has to perform the following diagnostic function:
   - He has to assess the entry behaviour of the students. He has to diagnose the initial potential of the learner in terms of cognitive, conative and affective abilities of the students. He has to identify and formulate specific objectives, the types and amount of behavioural changes he wants to introduce in the students.
   - The teacher has to have a clear picture of the individual differences among the learners.
   - The teacher has to undertake a task analysis by analysing the content, instructional material and facilities available.The teacher has to diagnose his own potential and capabilities and bring desirable improvement in his own behaviour for the successful completion of the teaching-learning process.
2. *Prescriptive Functions:* On the basis of the diagnosis, the teacher takes decisions about the action to be taken in order to complete the task. Fulfillment of objectives calls for an interaction between the teacher and the student which in turn needs proper management of the intervening variables by the teacher. For this to happen the teacher performs the following functions:
   - The teacher selects appropriate contents and organises them into a proper sequence.
   - Keeping in mind the entry behaviour and individual differences between students, the teacher selects proper teaching techniques, strategies and feedback devices.

Tactics necessary for ensuring co-operation from students are to be chosen by the teacher.

3. *Evaluative Functions:* These functions pertain to the task of evaluating the progress and outcomes of the prescriptive functions which are measured in terms of realisation of the planned objectives:
   - The failure in the realisation of the objectives is essentially a failure in the prescriptive functions due to improper diagnosis or error in the implementation of them.
   - The various evaluation devices in the form of tests, observations, interviews, rating scales, inventories, and projective techniques are employed in this function. Here the student has to actively respond and evaluate his own progress in terms of behavioural changes and abilities acquired.
   - The teacher diagnoses his teaching effort on the basis of the student's response. He brings about necessary changes in his actions/teaching on the basis of feedback received.

## Phases of Teaching

The complex task of teaching makes it imperative on the part of the teacher to plan and execute it. The steps or stages are known as phases of teaching. They are:

- Pre-active phrase of teaching.
- Interactive phrase of teaching.
- Post-active phase of teaching.

### *Pre-active Phase of Teaching*

It is the phase of teaching associated with activities before the actual act of teaching takes place i.e., in short it is the planning phase of teaching. The objectives in this phase are:

*Fixation of Goals:* In this step the teacher formulates goals, aims and objectives. The teacher writes the objectives in specific terms in behavioural terms related to entry and terminal behaviours.

- Decision making about the subject matter.
- Arranging/sequencing the elements of content chosen for presentation.

- Deciding the strategies to be adopted while teaching.
- Sequencing the teaching strategies.

### *Interactive Phase of Teaching*

In the pre-active phase, activities are those that the teacher undertakes before entering the classroom. In the interactive phase teacher undertakes activities inside the classroom. The teacher provides students verbal stimulations of various kinds, makes explanations, asks questions, listens to student's responses and provides guidance. The activities in this phase are:

*Size up of the Class*: The teacher makes a mental picture of the class, the students by observation and face reading.

Diagnosis of the learners. The teacher by testing the previous knowledge assesses the abilities of learners, their academic background and interests and attitudes.

Reactive processes – Action – Reaction processes play the central role in the task of classroom interaction. For this purpose, teacher has to take right decisions with regard to the selection and use of the proper stimuli, schedule of enforcement and feedback devices and development of suitable strategies suiting to the needs of the student, teaching environment and teaching objectives.

Thus, in this phase of teaching an appropriate verbal and non-verbal interaction between the teacher and students is established by arranging suitable teaching-learning activities and an equally suitable and controlled classroom environment.

### *Post-Active Phase*

The third phase of the teaching act concerns with the evaluation activities. The teacher asks verbal or written form questions, to measure the achievement of the students. The activities are:

*Defining the exact dimensions of the changes caused by teaching:* The teacher compares the actual behaviour changes that have resulted with the expected behavioural changes. The teacher defines the criterion behaviour.

*Selecting appropriate testing devices and techniques:* The teacher selects testing devices that are both reliable and valid to evaluate the cognitive and non-cognitive aspects of the students. Depending on the need the teacher uses either criterion tests or performance tests.

Changing the strategies in terms of evidences gathered. Based on the feedback received from the test results the teacher can identify the lacunae / drawbacks or the highlights of his teaching. Based on the evaluation, if necessary modifications are planned for the next teaching-learning activity.

Thus, we can conclude that the process of teaching does not confine itself with mere classroom interaction or presentation of content, teaching material or learning experiences. We should realise that teaching is not only face-to-face dialogue between teacher and students. It begins even before the teacher enters the classroom and continues even after he leaves the classroom after completion of teaching. For effective teaching the teacher should plan and execute activities under all the three phases.

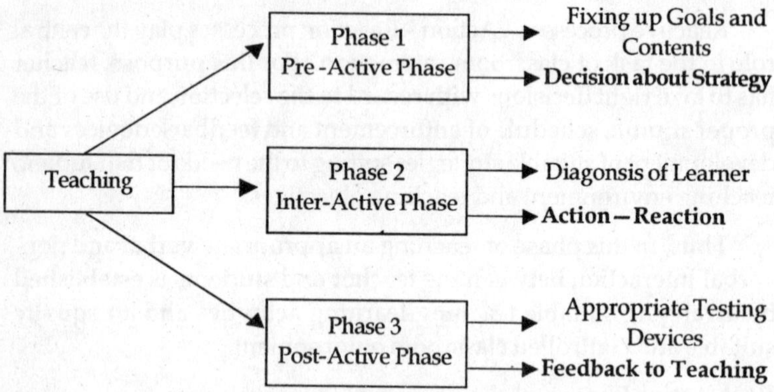


## LEVELS OF TEACHING

Teaching we all agree is a purposeful activity aimed at bringing about behavioural changes in the learner. In the classroom teaching-learning process involves a joint, co-operative task between the teacher and student. This teaching task takes place at various levels ranging from the least thoughtful and most thoughtful mode of action. Psychologists and educationists have clearly identified three levels of teaching-learning act namely memory level, understanding level and reflecting level.

Memory level falls at the bottom (or on a three-point rating scale at the extreme left) depicting the involvement of least thoughtful behaviour and reflective level at the top needing the involvement of higher cognitive abilities and most thoughtful behaviour. The understanding level falls in between, requiring a moderate amount of thoughtful behaviour.

### 1. *Memory Level of Teaching-Learning*

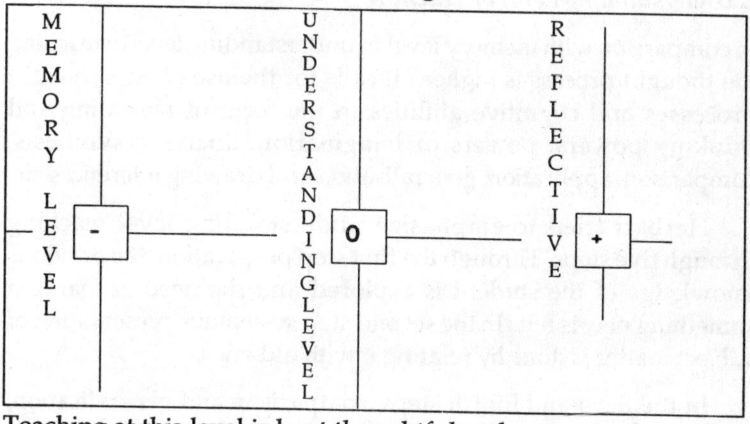


Teaching at this level is least thoughtful and memory plays a key role. Emphasis is placed as the presentation of facts and information and its organising. Thus, there is not much relation with intelligence as cramming is the point of focus in this level of teaching-learning and hence teaching lacks insight. The facts and information at cognitive level are supplied to the learner, which he stores in his brain, and recalls/recognises this knowledge when needed.

In memory level of teaching, the teacher is like a dictator who suppresses the independence, interests, attitudes and competencies of the student and tries to impose facts and information upon the students. Thus, the teacher remains active and in contrast the learners are passive receivers. The teaching-learning process is mechanical, one sided with practically no interaction i.e., it is teacher centered.

Signal learning, chain learning and stimulus – response learning is emphasised.

Further, the purpose of evaluation, traditional methods are used in the form of essay, short answer and objective type questions i.e., the student capacity to reproduce information is measured.

The motivation of learner is largely extrinsic. The learners engage themselves in memorisation of presented material due to external factors like fear of punishment, getting favour of teacher, passing a test or getting promotion to next grade.

The methods employed are exclusive teacher centered or subject centered – viz. lecture method, narration method etc.

**2. *Understanding Level of Teaching***

In comparison with memory level in understanding level of teaching the thought process is higher. It calls for the use of ones thought processes and cognitive abilities in the form of reasoning and thinking powers, powers of imagination, analysis, synthesis, comparison, application, generalisation and drawing inferences etc.

Herbart tried to emphasize understanding level teaching through five steps. Through the first step preparation, the previous knowledge of the student is explored and the need of learning something new is felt. In the second step systematic presentation of subject matter is done by relating it with old ones.

In the third and fourth steps, comparison and generalisation, students are supposed to identify common elements in the presented material/factual information and make generalization in the form of generalized facts, rule or principle. In step five applications, they are supposed to make use of the generalized principle by applying it to new situations.

The teacher plays a dominant and authoritarian role in this level of teaching. The teacher takes care that the student gains complete mastery of the subject matter in terms of its full understanding and generalized insight than in its mere memorization i.e., retention and reproduction. The learner is relatively more active than in memory level but still has to act within the framework set up by the teacher. The motivation is extrinsic as in the case of memory level. The teacher uses lecture-demonstration, question-answer types of methods to develop knowledge and understanding. The evaluation procedures adopted make use of tests to know the student's ability to analyse, synthesise, compare, generalise and apply to new situation.

**3. *Reflective Level Teaching***

This level of teaching includes both understanding and memory-level teaching. Essentially reflective level means 'Problem – Centered' teaching. It represents the highest level of the teaching-learning act that can be carried out at the most thoughtful modes of operation providing the desirable quality of teaching-learning situation and experiences to the learner for utilizing and enhancing their cognitive abilities to the maximum. It provides opportunities for the learner to utilise his cognitive abilities. It is nothing but a problem solving or discovery approach towards teaching-learning process.

Reflective teaching has its roots in the cognitive field theory of learning. It emphasize upon the learning of generalized insight, ways of discovering the facts and acquiring the skill of problem solving. The content is presented in an open-minded, problem solving form and is not structured as in memory/understanding level.

The teacher assumes the role of a guide. He does not play a dominant role. He helps student to discover facts or generalisations and does not present facts. The learner cannot remain a passive listener or silent observer; he has to make use of his cognitive abilities in solving the problem in hand. The student has intrinsic motivation and is filled with curiosity to learn for his own personal satisfaction.

The methods used are student centered like discovery, problem solving, analytic method etc. Evaluation procedures are used to test their problem solving ability, ingenuity or creativity etc.

**Comparative Study of Different Levels of Teaching-Learning**

| *Characteristic* | *Memory Level* | *Understanding Level* | *Reflective Level* |
|---|---|---|---|
| **Mode of Operation** | Least thoughtful | Moderately thoughtful | Most thoughtful |
| **Underlying Psychological Theories** | Theory of mental discipline, Herbartian Apperception mass theory, Thorndike's Connectionism & Theory of Conditioning | Herbartian five steps of Teaching & Learning, Gestalt field theory or Theory of Insight learning | Cognitive field Theory of Learning |
| **Main Objective** | Knowledge To acquire knowledge of facts theories & information | Understanding to acquire the knowledge with full understanding and | Understanding & creativity to understand the acquired facts with increased |

*(Contd.)*

| *Characteristic* | *Memory Level* | *Understanding Level* | *Reflective Level* |
|---|---|---|---|
| | | generalised insights | ability to reflect and discover new insights leading to independent problem solving |
| **Nature of subject matter and its organisation** | Structured, Organised and pre-planned; Systematic presentation of Factual information | Structured, Organised and preplanned; Meaningful and sequential presentation leading to generalisation and application | Unstructured and open ended; problem centered presentation. |
| **Role of the teacher** | Dominant and Authoritarian; Mere exposition without bothering for learner participation & understanding | Dominant and Authoritarian; Providing knowledge ensuring full understanding of learner | Democratic and Cooperative; Helping learner in reflective thinking and problem solving |
| **Nature of Motivation** | Extrinsic | Extrinsic | Intrinsic |
| **Methods Employed & their Nature** | Subject and teacher centered leading to rote learning | Subject centered leading to meaning full learning | Learner centered and Problem centered leading to problem solving and discovery learning |
| **Classroom Environment** | Quiet dull, One way communication with no interaction at all | Moderate in terms of interaction with major role for teacher | Quite healthy, lively interaction, providing for reflective thinking and constructive interaction |
| **Evaluation Devices Used** | Oral and written, Recall & Recognise type questions for testing memorisation power | Oral, written and practical, objective and short-answer type questions for testing knowledge and understanding | Oral, written and practical, essay types questions or open-ended questions for testing originality, creativity & problem solving ability. |

## Teaching and Related Terms

Terms like conditioning, training, instruction and indoctrination are used to denote some other kinds of teaching. At times they are even used as synonyms for teaching. But each of these though denote one or other types of teaching, they are inherently different. Teaching is a larger concept and each of these is a part or aspect of this large concept.

***(a) Teaching***

Teaching, as a whole is aimed to bring about changes in the behaviour of the students. These changes are brought about by –

- Teaching them how to perform a task.
- Teaching them how to respond to a situation or stimuli.
- Teaching them those aspects that contribute to their enrichment of knowledge.

Shaping their behaviour, attitudes and beliefs in teaching, an interaction occurs between the teacher and the students as a result of which students are diverted towards the planned objectives. Let us now discuss about the different modes of teaching.

***(b) Conditioning***

It is the lowest level or mode of teaching. A dog may be conditioned to lift its paw when it hears a bell. Similarly we may be taught to respond to signals, alarms, signs and warnings through conditioning. Most of our desirable or undesirable behaviours and habits are the creation of the process of conditioning. Ex: Saying excuse me when we sneeze etc.

***(c) Training***

It is at a higher level of teacher when compared to conditioning. It helps in shaping conduct and teaching various skills. In the circus animals are trained for specific tasks. Similarly we are trained in the use of machines and gadgets – their operations etc., with training less intelligent or simple behaviour are produced and in comparison teaching produces higher intelligence behaviour.

***(d) Instruction***

Instruction is mainly concerned with the development of knowledge and understanding in an individual about a thing, system or process. Instruction caters towards the development of intellect and affects the cognitive domain of ones behaviour. In comparison teaching is aimed towards shaping a total man including cognitive and affective domains with the cognitive domain.

Another aspect is the presence of teacher. In instruction the human instructor can be replaced by computer, teaching machine programmed material, radio, television, video etc. But teaching necessarily involves face-to-face interaction. In teaching, teacher can use any of the aids mentioned above to enhance his teaching.

### *(e) Indoctrination*

It refers to the transmission of doctrine, firm faith or system of beliefs. It represents a fairly high level of teaching which leads to the establishment or shaping of beliefs and ideals.

It requires higher order of intelligence and results in bringing quite stable changes in the cognitive and affective domains of ones behaviour.

Let us now compare the four modes of teaching conditioning, training, instruction and indoctrination.

| *Aspect* | *Conditioning* | *Training* | *Instructing* | *Indoctrination* |
|---|---|---|---|---|
| Purpose | Shaping behaviour | Shaping skills and behaviour | Transmitting knowledge | Shaping beliefs |
| Teaching aim | Making some to do as something as one desires | Teaching some one how to do something | Teaching some one that this is the way to do something | Teaching some one that so and so is the only way of doing it |
| Objective | Formation of habit | Formation of skills | Formation of knowledge | Formation of attitudes, beliefs |
| Domain | Psychomotor | Psychomotor | Cognitive | Affective |
| Type of Learning | Signal Learning | Chain Learning | Concept Learning | Principle Learning |
| Level of Learning | Thoughtless – Memory Level | Thoughtless – Memory Level | Thoughtful – Understanding level | Thoughtful – Reflective level |
| Nature | Memorisation | Performance | Response | Reflection |
| Example | Teaching alphabets, symbols | Developing speaking, reading skills | Teaching concepts, theories principles | Developing attitudes, beliefs, feelings |
| Application | Small children | Training for certain acts | Teaching at higher level | Higher level teaching |
| Outcome | Behaviour shaping | Conduct shaping | Knowledge transmission | Belief and Value formation |

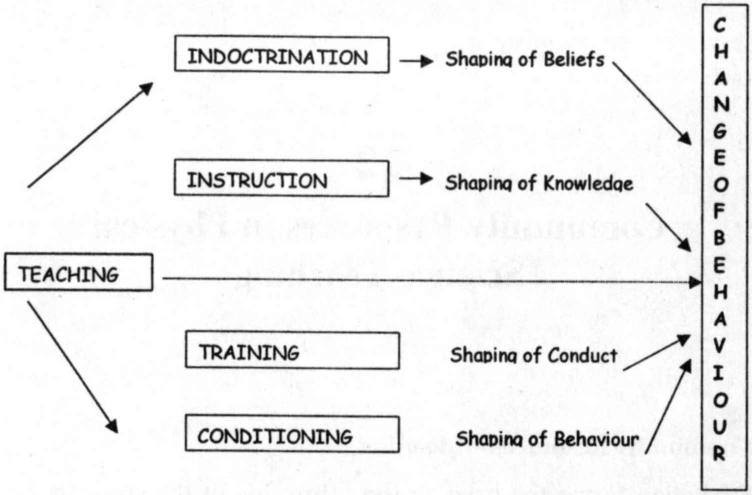
INDOCTRINATION
Shaping of Beliefs
INSTRUCTION
Shaping of Knowledge
TEACHING
TRAINING
Shaping of Conduct
CONDITIONING
Shaping of Behaviour
CHANGE OF BEHAVIOUR

# 12

# Community Resources in Physical Science Teaching

## Community Resources – Meaning

Education forms the basis to the future life of the students. So education should be useful for both students as well as the Society. In tune with this, besides scientific knowledge, to solve life problems, it will be of no use by following the present procedures. That means, by teaching the content in a detailed manner, the student sits passively and cannot listen. So there will be no use in these methods of teaching. Even then, to have this method of teaching in practice, can you guess the reason why this method is in implementation? For a developing country like ours, the resources and equipment needed to teach physical sciences is not available in the school premises. To teach physical sciences in an effective manner, economic constraints need not become the hurdle. Though ours is a poor country we should not forget that there are plenty of resources in our country. That is why we should correlate the curriculum with the resources and then to be taught. We know the tremendous effects in these trails at this stage. Only then the children can learn many interesting things of the outside world. Moreover, children learn the things in a perfect manner by the Principle of learningand by Living. You should know how the child learns the skills required for life. The child associates himself with the surroundings by utilizing the available resources for teaching-learning process. Only with this, all these things are possible. That means minimizing the gap between community and school, these two units together to work thoroughly understanding the society and utilizing it for teaching, serving the society and making the society to participate in teaching-learning process. That is the idea underlying in the aim of utilizing the resources available within the community though they are outside the school premises.

**The Objectives of Utilizing the Community Resources**

The following are the objectives of utilizing the community resources in teaching:

1. Providing the knowledge of the lessons to be learnt well in advance to the students.
2. Collecting the necessary teaching-learning materials and resources needed to the topic of teaching.
3. Developing the creativity, power of observation and intuitive capacity.
4. We all know that perfect learning takes place through observation of natural phenomenon. So for learning, nature and natural process and their utility is of utmost importance.
5. Special interests can be inculcated among students by utilizing these resources.
6. Relating the resources to classroom teaching and the curriculum.
7. Providing the specific information related to the topic, social resources should be considered.
8. To teach any topic it is better to provide direct exposure. Even for those topics learnt in classroom also it is possible to utilize the resources to make it more clear and elaborate.
9. We know that in the present system of education, both curricular and co-curricular activities have special significance. This is possible only through utilizing the community resources.

**The Reason for Utilizing the Community Resources**

Toys are useful to explain the scientific facts, use of the concepts and their inquiry among the things used by children. In this manner, children are motivated to learn science in a situational manner. Due to this, there is place in every activity and in the classroom and outside the laboratory, there are so many possibilities to learn the scientific concepts. To brief science teacher should use the community resources in an intelligent manner. We will see the reasons for this.

Science teaching can be made more effective by using different resources and equipment. But many resources required for teaching science and equipment are available in plenty in our near by environment.

Only our direct experiences facilitate to get clear understanding of representative experiences.

1. It is always better to use more aids in the teaching-learning process. For this utilization of resources is more helpful. If we use these types of approaches talented do not get bored and slow learners understand better.
2. It is possible to learn the scientific concept quickly by real experience.
3. To make the abstract things concrete, we need community resources.
4. Science has its application not only in abstract concepts of science laboratories but also in every human activity in day-to-day life situations.
5. There is possibility to get the resources from the community if they are not available in schools. The skill of problem solving, keen observation etc. can be effectively developed by the use of community resources outside the school i.e., outer world.
6. There is possibility of wide span of social life through scientific reforms.
7. Strengthening of school community relationship is also an important factor in this direction.
8. It creates interest among the children if they are taken out for a visit or using different resources instead of routine way of teaching.
9. The students understand the relationship between the knowledge taught in the class and the society where the knowledge is put into practice.
10. The students get first hand experience.

**Types of Resources**

The community resources in science teaching can be categorized in 3 types.

Physical surroundings like tanks, seas, lakes, rivers, hills, streams, earthquakes, floods, factories, industries, paddy fields, forests etc.

Live stock like animals, birds, vegetation, zoos, where these are exhibited, agricultural fields, animal husbandaries, poultries, diary farms, veterinary hospitals.

The experts in the community like different occupational groups, artisans, engineers, doctors, lawyers, professors, nurses, technicians, veterinary doctors, mechanics etc.

**Methods of Utilizing Community Resources**

In Physical Science Teaching, community resources can be utilized in 3 ways. They are:

To bring the varied type of community resources into the classroom.

- If there are experts in different fields in the vicinity, lectures or talks can be arranged on these topics or the children can be taken to their place of work like railway station, ice factory, satellite launching station etc.
- Arranging the field trips and excursions to the places of scientific importance like exhibitions, science centres, planetarium etc. The teacher should maintain a source file indicating the place, persons having scientific knowledge, institutions like banks, railway stations, school buildings, hospitals, garden, forests, water supply system, radio broadcasting, T.V. stations, dams, poultries, diary farm etc.

First we will see how the available things in our surroundings can be used as community resources:

The child lives in the physical surroundings and the child is also part of the physical environment. That means the child throughout his/her life interacts with the surroundings. So the surroundings of the child includes both the environment in which he/she lives, the conditions familiar or unfamiliar, physical, social process etc. either directly or indirectly influence the child. So varied types of interaction among different living beings can be said as example. The formation of islands, deposits of salts in the soil, drought or famine, floods etc. are the interaction between non-living things and living things.

World itself is the biggest laboratory. So the experiments can be conducted in this laboratory with full self-confidence and without any fear. We use the sense organs to acquire knowledge of the nature. But sometimes these sense organs fail to receive reliable information. For Ex. Bacteria, we cannot see the micro-organisms like protozoa etc. with the naked eyes. To observe these, compound microscope is required. Similarly to observe stars or ellipses, which are very big and far away from our reach, we need telescope. So microscopes, telescopes help us to study minute or largest objects respectively. That means our senses fail to grasp the correct information from the nature. Thus to study natural phenomenon, some scientific equipment is necessary. If the teacher wants to provide sensory training to the children, it is necessary to provide opportunity to the child to interact frequently with the physical surroundings. In addition to this, the teacher should try to use the materials available with environment in the teaching-learning process to the maximum extent. That does not mean that the teacher should spend money to collect these things. While teaching a particular lesson, it is possible to motivate the children to discover the natural process by explaining the situations actually happened in their surroundings. So both in teaching physical science and creating interest among children, utilization of available resources helps in making teaching much more interesting and natural in providing first hand experience to students.

By studying the things like animals living in the surroundings, fossils, soils, minerals and so on the skills like observation, collection, classification of objects etc. can be developed among children. Added to this by observing the seasonal variations, it is possible for the children to plan their life in an orderly manner suited to these changes. The concepts can be developed by observing the place, time and mutual relationship between there two. To teach the biosphere, the life patterns, the resources of the society like forests, water tanks, lakes etc. can be made use of. Through interaction with the surroundings, the direct experience of the child widens the scope of the knowledge (known to unknown, concrete to abstract, specific to general aspect). For this arrangement of excursions and field trips have scientific importance and the nature can be brought closer to the child. These experiences prepare the students to face the realities of the life.

Family, social life, interaction between different organisms etc. become part and parcel of child's social environment. Usually child spends more time in the family. The student should face the ups and downs of the social environment. Similarly the child has physical and economic resources. So it is necessary to train the students to interact with the social and economic environment in a planned manner.

**Resources to be Used from Social Environment**

Locally in the vicinity of the school, there are number of people with suitable qualifications and expertise in different fields. For Ex. We see people having in depth knowledge in the field of art, painting, music, carpentry, agriculture etc. in our society. Pupils appreciate if lectures, exhibitions are arranged on the topics related to science curriculum by these people. These conditions provide opportunity for the children to clarify the doubts if any in those areas of knowledge. Sometimes this may require in depth knowledge for which the teacher is helpless to clarify the doubts of students.

The duty of the teacher is to teach in an efficient manner. But at the same time the teacher cannot provide the skills of other professions among children. It can be made possible to utilize the services of the experts in the society to teach the topics like work experience, professional skills etc. It is always appreciable to share the knowledge and skills between the school and surrounding society. Unless education becomes a social process and people of the society show some concern in the school activities. Otherwise the parents do not have confidence in the school system.

Various organizations came into existence for smooth running of the society. So there is every possibility to utilize the Government and non-government staff working in the organizations while teaching physical sciences. For Ex. Human body, health, hygiene, nutrition, inferiority complex etc., can be taught efficiently by the local doctor or nurse or a health worker. Similarly to teach modern agricultural methods, high yielding varieties, manures, the method of using fertilizers and pesticides, post-harvest technology etc. the services of village agricultural offices the services of extension officers can be made use of. It is highly appreciable it in the school time table at least one period in a week must be allotted for speeches of such persons or such insist to strengthen the school and community relationship.

**Mobile Services**

In the recent past, mobile services are complementing the institutions. Mobile vehicles are the useful means for propagating the scientific knowledge in the rural areas. Mobile library, mobile family control unit, student mobile van used by NCERT to reach remote rural and hilly areas with science kits. This vehicle goes to different schools and provide the necessary guidance to these students in science. The services of these mobile vehicles should be utilized when these mobile vans go to the schools. In Tamil Nadu a polytechnic institute prepared a mobile science vehicle with a mini laboratory to work in rural areas. In the same manner Visweswaraiah Industrial and Technological Museum also prepared 12 mobile units. In these units trained personnel in science go to the rural schools and conduct relevant experiments in physical sciences and show to the students of 9 and 10 classes. So the teacher should also try to utilize the services of these mobile vans. Recently even the Government of AP started the efforts to introduce the mobile laboratories in vehicle to expose science to rural school children and inculcate awareness.

# 13

# Computers in Teaching Physical Sciences

## Introduction to Computers

Computer is a device or a machine like radio, tape recorder, T.V. etc. The word 'computer' is originated from the word 'Compute'. Compute means to count. So in the broader sense, computer can be called 'Computing Machine'. Due to the revolution in the field of computers, computer is not confined only to count, but it is expanded to many more fields, works and activities. It is a well-known fact that it can be used for so many purposes. To mention a few, in engineering, designing, commerce, medicine, sports, astronomical research, sending greetings to people in other countries, booking the railway tickets, giving knowledge of music to music lovers, helping deaf and dumb etc. Thus, the usage of computers is not confined to this or that field. It is being used in almost every field of knowledge. To tell in a word, in this modern age, our multiple needs can be catered through multimedia approach of computer. In this manner, computer is the most efficient device performing numerous tasks and innumerable activities. But it works only in accordance with the instructions given by the operator. It cannot think on its own or decide as per the requirement as it is only a machine.

Now you will be familiarized with some words related to computers.

1. Computer hardware includes machine, its equipment and its parts. We can touch and sense them.
2. Keyboard, printer, screen, floppy, CD can be mentioned as hardware.

3. Computer software means the instructions given to function the machine in the form of computer language. This also can be called programme. This is neither touched nor seen. The computer languages viz. Basic, COBOL, GIS etc. can be considered as software. By utilising the software developed by us, this will serve our needs with the maximum speed with greater accuracy and less effort. Based on the information given i.e. the input, controls and operates in a specific manner, the required information is stored in the memory and gives out whenever it is required. Thus it is useful in a number of ways. It follows our instructions, answers our questions, work as per the instructions and provides the results. This is known as output. All this is the basic common explanation about computers. This can be shown figuratively as follows:

The software used in Computer Assisted instruction is of 2 types.

1. Application software, and
2. System software.

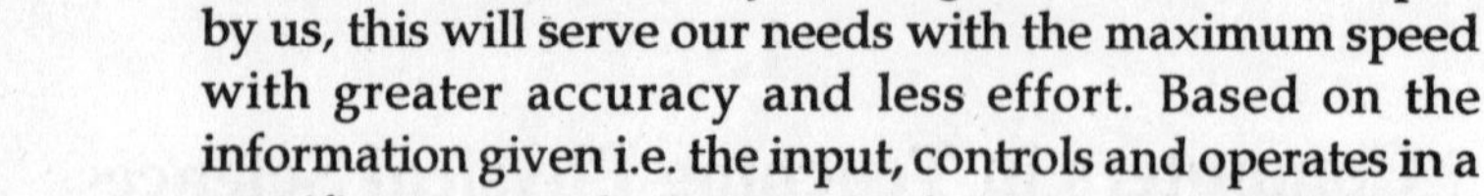


1. *The Application Software:* The instructions given to the Computers in the form of programme to get the work required by the users are known as application software.
2. *The System Software:* The Computer resources necessary to carryout the application activities are called the system software.

A machine, which has the capacity to follow instructions and function and control, can be called a 'Computer'.

**Role of Computers in Teaching Physical Sciences**

Here you will learn how computers help in physical science teaching. To store the information related to physical science, to utilize the information whenever required, to make the changes as per the requirement and to get the information in verbal, tabular and figurative manner. That means history, knowledge of physical sciences, research information, details of the studies of the scientists, model of modern equipment, the details of researches of the present era, their results etc. with the internet the entire world can be brought before us. It is possible only with this instrument to come in to contact with the entire world in a few seconds.

Secondly, it is an acceptable fact that the student learns according to the interest, efficiency, intelligence etc. So programmed learning is possible with the Computers. Moreover, it improves the knowledge of the student. From this we can estimate the importance of machine i.e. computer in individualized instruction and learning process.

Thirdly, complex phenomenon of physical sciences, its theories, its principles can be drilled for better learning. It can be made flexible for thorough practice of concepts already learnt. With this machine, based on the individual efficiency, with repeated practice we can prepare perfectly trained personnel.

In this way, this is only an example to understand the life experiences in the physical environment to understand the information in a scientific manner, individualized instruction, stimulation, learning and achievement through play way techniques, in so many ways in the modern living, helping the officials to provide coordinated governance etc. For Ex. Our Chief Minister Sri Chandrababu Naidu discusses with officials on video and teleconferences, EdCET counselling, recently started telemedicine etc. There is no necessity to tell that all these developments come under this category. This type of development is possible only by integrating different media. To achieve all such developments, science is playing the key role.

## Different Computers in Physical Science Teaching

### *Class Project*

To use the computer having varied types of utility and uses, there are various governmental funded educational fields. A pilot project was launched in 1984-85 by the Department of Electronics and Ministry of Human Resource Development. But in 1993-94 based on the recommendations of Finance Ministry it was changed into centrally sponsored scheme. Presently this scheme is under implementation to senior secondary stage i.e., 11 and 12 class students. This is under the control of compulsory literacy education, the secretary as its president. This scheme is being implemented and supervised by National Steering Committee at 500 centres in central provinces.

**Computer Aided Instruction (CAI)**

Computer Aided Teaching or Computer Aided Instruction is a programmed method based on the principle of teaching by considering the individual differences of students by storing the information in an orderly manner and giving back to them. This was first introduced in Illinois University of America in the year 1961 by the programme 'Plato'. After that Patric Supson used it as a supplement in teaching reading and arithmetic to school children at Stanford University. This type of computer aided instruction is really a boon in coping with the changing scenario of this modern education system and its varied needs.

**Multimedia**

The word multi refers to more than one. Thus multimedia conveys that more than one medium. That is in other words putting different media together. With the integration of different media, multimedia came into existence. That means it is the combination of audio-visual information and animation. We can come in to contact with the entire world with the use of internet. For example, Video conference, teleconference, e-mail, E-commerce, E-marketing etc. belong to this type of developmental schemes.

This multimedia is helpful to prepare different Compact Discs (CDs) mostly available in different subjects according to the interests and needs of the students. The video conference is very much useful to collect information from well-trained and expert people. This facility lays an important foundation to change the thinking patterns and sharpening the young minds besides enhancing creative ability of the children. Listening to music, playing, drawing, answering etc. i.e. different activities can be attended simultaneously. We can down load the information already stored from the internet which includes pictures, photographs, graphs, verbal information, etc. Sounds can also be incorporated to make the teaching more lively. All this is possible only because of "WINDOWS".

**Merits in Using Computers**

1. The teachers and students can save their time by using computers in teaching-learning process.
2. The students become sharp in their thinking.
3. The knowledge of the students will become broadened.

4. It connects the entire world in a fraction of second.
5. It the teacher uses colour monitors and sounds, it almost resembles the original. So it will be an effective multimedia aid in teaching-learning process.

**Limitations Inusing Computers**

1. It is very expensive to establish computers in all the schools.
2. By using the computers in teaching-learning process, human relations will not be properly developed.
3. It is very difficult to use computer aided instruction by all the teachers at all times for all topics.
4. The use of computers needs trained teachers in developing the lessons by using computers.
5. The small screen may not be suitable to teach the students in big classrooms and large size. So it may not be feasible to be used in classroom settings.
6. The teachers should be familiar with its parts, functions besides its repair if something goes wrong. So it is difficult to operate.
7. It is a time consuming process to make the students to operate the computers on their own.
8. It is frequently changing field. Again and again it requires new knowledge whenever there is a change in the model, its functions etc. of the computer.

## SUGGESTED REFERENCES

1. Amit Kumar—"Teaching Physical Sciences", Anmol Publications Pvt. Ltd., New Delhi, 1995.
2. Anju Soni—"Teaching of Science", Tandon Publications, Ludhiana, 2000.
3. Siddiqi and Siddiqi—"Teaching of Science Today and Tomorrow", Doaba House, New Delhi, 1998.
4. R. C. Sharma—"Modern Science Teaching", Dhanpat Rai and Sons, New Delhi, 1987.
5. R. C. Das—"Science Teaching in Schools", Sterling Publishers Pvt. Ltd., New Delhi, 1990.
6. Narendra Vaidya—"The Impact Science Teaching", Oxford and IBH Publishing Co. Pvt. Ltd., 1989.
7. Rajeev Garg —"World Famous Scientists", Pustak Mahal, New Delhi, 1994.
8. D. V. R. Bhaskahra Sastry, C. N. V. Subba Rao—"Vignanna Sastramulo Dhruvatharalu", Telugu Academy, Hyderabad, 2001.

9. Nagasuri Venugopal—"Science Vaitalikulu", Sree Madhulatha Publications, Vijayawads, 2002.

The following URLs have been referred to get the information about scientists and more information can be obtained in these sites.

1. http://www.history.mcs.standrews.ac.uk/history/Mathematicians /He is enberg.html
2. http://www.nobel.se/physics/laureates.html
3. http://www.nobel.se/physics/laureates/1983/chandrasekharau tobio./html
4. http://galileo. imss. firenze. it/museo/4/eiv06.html
5. http://www.scienceworld. wolfram.com/physics.html
6. http://www.encyclopedia.com

# Bibliography


1. Amit Kumar (1995), "Teaching Physical Sciences", Anmol Publications Pvt. Ltd., New Delhi.
2. Anju Soni (2000), "Teaching of Science", Tandon Publications, Ludhiana.
3. Siddiqi and Siddiqi (1998), 'Teaching of Science Today and Tomorrow', Doaba House, New Delhi.
4. R. C. Sharma (1987), 'Modern Science Teaching', Dhanpat Rai and Sons, New Delhi.
5. R. C. Das (1990), 'Science Teaching in Schools', Sterling Publishers Pvt. Ltd., New Delhi.
6. Narendra Vaidya (1989), 'The Impact Science Teaching', Oxford and IBH Publishing Co. Pvt. Ltd.
7. Rajeev Garg (1994), 'World Famous Scientists', Pustak Mahal, New Delhi.
8. D. V. R. Bhaskahra Sastry, C. N. V. Subba Rao (2001), "Vignanna Sastramulo Dhruvatharalu", Telugu Academy, Hyderabad.
9. Nagasuri Venugopal (2002), 'Science Vaitalikulu', Sree Madhulatha Publications,Vijayawada.
10. Vanaja, M. (2004), 'Methods of Teaching Physical Sciences', Neelkamal Publications, Hyderabad.
11. SPMVV (2003), 'Self-learning Material for Methods of Teaching Physical Sciences for B.Ed. Students', SPMVV, Tirupati.


The following URLs have been referred to get the information about scientists and more information can be obtained in these sites:

1. http://www.history.mcs.standrews.ac.uk/history/Mathematicians/He is enberg.html
2. http://www.nobel.se/physics/laureates.html
3 http://www.nobel.se/physics/laureates/1983/chandrasekharautobio./html
4. http://galileo. imss. firenze. it/museo/4/eiv06.html
5. http://www.scienceworld. wolfram.com/physics.html
6. http://www.encyclopedia.com

# Index